The Spiritual Whistleblower Presents:

MY
LOOSH
JOURNAL

D1567245

Chanel J. Clark
PO Box 20486
New York, NY 10009

ISBN-9798572916560

Printed in the United States of America

Date: ___/___/___

How are you feeling today? (Angry/*Depressed/Happy/Indifferent/Sick*)

_____
_____
_____
_____
_____
_____

Did you receive a Hoover from the Narcissist today? If yes, how did you respond?

_____
_____
_____
_____
_____

List a small goal that you will work towards accomplishing tomorrow:

_____
_____
_____
_____
_____

Date: ___/___/___

How are you feeling today? (Angry/*Depressed/Happy/Indifferent/Sick*)

_____

_____

_____

_____

_____

_____

_____

Did you receive a Hoover from the Narcissist today? If yes, how did you respond?

_____

_____

_____

_____

_____

_____

List a small goal that you will work towards accomplishing tomorrow:

_____

_____

_____

_____

_____

_____

Date: ___/___/___

How are you feeling today? (Angry/*Depressed*/*Happy*/*Indifferent*/*Sick*)

_____

_____

_____

_____

_____

_____

Did you receive a Hoover from the Narcissist today? If yes, how did you respond?

_____

_____

_____

_____

_____

List a small goal that you will work towards accomplishing tomorrow:

_____

_____

_____

_____

_____

_____

Date: ___/___/___

How are you feeling today? (Angry/*Depressed*/*Happy*/*Indifferent*/*Sick*)

_____

_____

_____

_____

_____

_____

_____

Did you receive a Hoover from the Narcissist today? If yes, how did you respond?

_____

_____

_____

_____

_____

_____

List a small goal that you will work towards accomplishing tomorrow:

_____

_____

_____

_____

_____

_____

Date: ___/___/___

How are you feeling today? (Angry/*Depressed/Happy/Indifferent/Sick*)

_____

_____

_____

_____

_____

_____

Did you receive a Hoover from the Narcissist today? If yes, how did you respond?

_____

_____

_____

_____

_____

List a small goal that you will work towards accomplishing tomorrow:

_____

_____

_____

_____

_____

Date: ___/___/___

How are you feeling today? (Angry/*Depressed*/*Happy*/*Indifferent*/*Sick*)

_____

_____

_____

_____

_____

_____

Did you receive a Hoover from the Narcissist today? If yes, how did you respond?

_____

_____

_____

_____

_____

List a small goal that you will work towards accomplishing tomorrow:

_____

_____

_____

_____

_____

_____

Date: ___/___/___

How are you feeling today? (Angry/*Depressed*/*Happy*/*Indifferent*/*Sick*)

_____

_____

_____

_____

_____

_____

Did you receive a Hoover from the Narcissist today? If yes, how did you respond?

_____

_____

_____

_____

_____

List a small goal that you will work towards accomplishing tomorrow:

_____

_____

_____

_____

_____

Date: ___/___/___

How are you feeling today? (Angry/*Depressed/Happy/Indifferent/Sick*)

_____

_____

_____

_____

_____

_____

_____

Did you receive a Hoover from the Narcissist today? If yes, how did you respond?

_____

_____

_____

_____

_____

List a small goal that you will work towards accomplishing tomorrow:

_____

_____

_____

_____

_____

_____

Date: ___/___/___

How are you feeling today? (Angry/*Depressed/Happy/Indifferent/Sick*)

_____

_____

_____

_____

_____

_____

Did you receive a Hoover from the Narcissist today? If yes, how did you respond?

_____

_____

_____

_____

_____

List a small goal that you will work towards accomplishing tomorrow:

_____

_____

_____

_____

_____

"If you wait by the river long enough, the bodies of your enemies will float by."

— Sun Tzu

"We must accept finite disappointment, but never lose infinite hope."

-MARTIN LUTHER KING JR.

Date: ___/___/___

How are you feeling today? (Angry/*Depressed*/*Happy*/*Indifferent*/*Sick*)

_____

_____

_____

_____

_____

_____

_____

Did you receive a Hoover from the Narcissist today? If yes, how did you respond?

_____

_____

_____

_____

_____

_____

_____

List a small goal that you will work towards accomplishing tomorrow:

_____

_____

_____

_____

_____

_____

_____

Date: ___/___/___

How are you feeling today? (Angry/*Depressed/Happy/Indifferent/Sick*)

_____

_____

_____

_____

_____

_____

Did you receive a Hoover from the Narcissist today? If yes, how did you respond?

_____

_____

_____

_____

_____

List a small goal that you will work towards accomplishing tomorrow:

_____

_____

_____

_____

_____

_____

Date: ___/___/___

How are you feeling today? (Angry/*Depressed/Happy/Indifferent/Sick*)

_____

_____

_____

_____

_____

_____

_____

Did you receive a Hoover from the Narcissist today? If yes, how did you respond?

_____

_____

_____

_____

_____

_____

List a small goal that you will work towards accomplishing tomorrow:

_____

_____

_____

_____

_____

_____

_____

Date: ___/___/___

How are you feeling today? (Angry/*Depressed/Happy/Indifferent/Sick*)

_____

_____

_____

_____

_____

_____

Did you receive a Hoover from the Narcissist today? If yes, how did you respond?

_____

_____

_____

_____

_____

List a small goal that you will work towards accomplishing tomorrow:

_____

_____

_____

_____

_____

Date: ___/___/___

How are you feeling today? (Angry/*Depressed*/*Happy*/*Indifferent*/*Sick*)

_____

_____

_____

_____

_____

_____

Did you receive a Hoover from the Narcissist today? If yes, how did you respond?

_____

_____

_____

_____

_____

List a small goal that you will work towards accomplishing tomorrow:

_____

_____

_____

_____

_____

Date: ___/___/___

How are you feeling today? (Angry/*Depressed/Happy/Indifferent/Sick*)

_____

_____

_____

_____

_____

_____

Did you receive a Hoover from the Narcissist today? If yes, how did you respond?

_____

_____

_____

_____

_____

List a small goal that you will work towards accomplishing tomorrow:

_____

_____

_____

_____

_____

Date: ___/___/___

How are you feeling today? (Angry/*Depressed*/*Happy*/*Indifferent*/*Sick*)

_____

_____

_____

_____

_____

_____

Did you receive a Hoover from the Narcissist today? If yes, how did you respond?

_____

_____

_____

_____

_____

_____

List a small goal that you will work towards accomplishing tomorrow:

_____

_____

_____

_____

_____

_____

Date: ___/___/___

How are you feeling today? (Angry/*Depressed/Happy/Indifferent/Sick*)

_____

_____

_____

_____

_____

_____

Did you receive a Hoover from the Narcissist today? If yes, how did you respond?

_____

_____

_____

_____

_____

List a small goal that you will work towards accomplishing tomorrow:

_____

_____

_____

_____

_____

Date: ___/___/___

How are you feeling today? (Angry/*Depressed/Happy/Indifferent/Sick*)

_____

_____

_____

_____

_____

_____

_____

Did you receive a Hoover from the Narcissist today? If yes, how did you respond?

_____

_____

_____

_____

_____

_____

List a small goal that you will work towards accomplishing tomorrow:

_____

_____

_____

_____

_____

_____

Date: ___/___/___

How are you feeling today? (Angry/*Depressed/Happy/Indifferent/Sick*)

_____

_____

_____

_____

_____

_____

_____

Did you receive a Hoover from the Narcissist today? If yes, how did you respond?

_____

_____

_____

_____

_____

List a small goal that you will work towards accomplishing tomorrow:

_____

_____

_____

_____

_____

Date: ___/___/___

How are you feeling today? (Angry/*Depressed*/*Happy*/*Indifferent*/*Sick*)

_____

_____

_____

_____

_____

_____

_____

Did you receive a Hoover from the Narcissist today? If yes, how did you respond?

_____

_____

_____

_____

_____

List a small goal that you will work towards accomplishing tomorrow:

_____

_____

_____

_____

_____

Date: ___/___/___

How are you feeling today? (Angry/*Depressed/Happy/Indifferent/Sick*)

_____

_____

_____

_____

_____

_____

Did you receive a Hoover from the Narcissist today? If yes, how did you respond?

_____

_____

_____

_____

_____

List a small goal that you will work towards accomplishing tomorrow:

_____

_____

_____

_____

Date: ___/___/___

How are you feeling today? (Angry/*Depressed*/*Happy*/*Indifferent*/*Sick*)

_____

_____

_____

_____

_____

_____

Did you receive a Hoover from the Narcissist today? If yes, how did you respond?

_____

_____

_____

_____

_____

List a small goal that you will work towards accomplishing tomorrow:

_____

_____

_____

_____

_____

Date: ___/___/___

How are you feeling today? (Angry/*Depressed/Happy/Indifferent/Sick*)

_____

_____

_____

_____

_____

_____

_____

Did you receive a Hoover from the Narcissist today? If yes, how did you respond?

_____

_____

_____

_____

_____

_____

List a small goal that you will work towards accomplishing tomorrow:

_____

_____

_____

_____

_____

Date: ___/___/___

How are you feeling today? (Angry/*Depressed*/*Happy*/*Indifferent*/*Sick*)

_____

_____

_____

_____

_____

_____

_____

Did you receive a Hoover from the Narcissist today? If yes, how did you respond?

_____

_____

_____

_____

_____

_____

List a small goal that you will work towards accomplishing tomorrow:

_____

_____

_____

_____

_____

_____

Date: ___/___/___

How are you feeling today? (Angry/*Depressed/Happy/Indifferent/Sick*)

_____

_____

_____

_____

_____

_____

Did you receive a Hoover from the Narcissist today? If yes, how did you respond?

_____

_____

_____

_____

_____

List a small goal that you will work towards accomplishing tomorrow:

_____

_____

_____

_____

_____

Date: ___/___/___

How are you feeling today? (Angry/*Depressed/Happy/Indifferent/Sick*)

_____

_____

_____

_____

_____

_____

_____

Did you receive a Hoover from the Narcissist today? If yes, how did you respond?

_____

_____

_____

_____

_____

_____

List a small goal that you will work towards accomplishing tomorrow:

_____

_____

_____

_____

_____

Date: ___/___/___

How are you feeling today? (Angry/*Depressed/Happy/Indifferent/Sick*)

_____

_____

_____

_____

_____

_____

Did you receive a Hoover from the Narcissist today? If yes, how did you respond?

_____

_____

_____

_____

_____

_____

List a small goal that you will work towards accomplishing tomorrow:

_____

_____

_____

_____

_____

Date: ___/___/___

How are you feeling today? (Angry/*Depressed/Happy/Indifferent/Sick*)

_____

_____

_____

_____

_____

_____

_____

Did you receive a Hoover from the Narcissist today? If yes, how did you respond?

_____

_____

_____

_____

_____

List a small goal that you will work towards accomplishing tomorrow:

_____

_____

_____

_____

_____

Date: ___/___/___

How are you feeling today? (Angry/*Depressed/Happy/Indifferent/Sick*)

_____

_____

_____

_____

_____

_____

Did you receive a Hoover from the Narcissist today? If yes, how did you respond?

_____

_____

_____

_____

_____

List a small goal that you will work towards accomplishing tomorrow:

_____

_____

_____

_____

Date: ___/___/___

How are you feeling today? (Angry/*Depressed/Happy/Indifferent/Sick*)

_____

_____

_____

_____

_____

_____

Did you receive a Hoover from the Narcissist today? If yes, how did you respond?

_____

_____

_____

_____

_____

List a small goal that you will work towards accomplishing tomorrow:

_____

_____

_____

_____

_____

Date: ___/___/___

How are you feeling today? (Angry/*Depressed/Happy/Indifferent/Sick*)

_____

_____

_____

_____

_____

_____

_____

Did you receive a Hoover from the Narcissist today? If yes, how did you respond?

_____

_____

_____

_____

_____

_____

List a small goal that you will work towards accomplishing tomorrow:

_____

_____

_____

_____

_____

_____

"When you're at the end of your rope, tie a knot and hold on."

-THEODORE ROOSEVELT

"Hope is being able to see that there is light despite all of the darkness."

-DESMOND TUTU

Date: ___/___/___

How are you feeling today? (Angry/*Depressed*/*Happy*/*Indifferent*/*Sick*)

_____

_____

_____

_____

_____

_____

_____

Did you receive a Hoover from the Narcissist today? If yes, how did you respond?

_____

_____

_____

_____

_____

_____

List a small goal that you will work towards accomplishing tomorrow:

_____

_____

_____

_____

_____

_____

_____

Date: ___/___/___

How are you feeling today? (Angry/*Depressed/Happy/Indifferent/Sick*)

_____

_____

_____

_____

_____

_____

Did you receive a Hoover from the Narcissist today? If yes, how did you respond?

_____

_____

_____

_____

_____

List a small goal that you will work towards accomplishing tomorrow:

_____

_____

_____

_____

_____

_____

Date: ___/___/___

How are you feeling today? (Angry/*Depressed/Happy/Indifferent/Sick*)

_____

_____

_____

_____

_____

_____

Did you receive a Hoover from the Narcissist today? If yes, how did you respond?

_____

_____

_____

_____

_____

List a small goal that you will work towards accomplishing tomorrow:

_____

_____

_____

_____

_____

_____

Date: ___/___/___

How are you feeling today? (Angry/*Depressed/Happy/Indifferent/Sick*)

_____

_____

_____

_____

_____

_____

Did you receive a Hoover from the Narcissist today? If yes, how did you respond?

_____

_____

_____

_____

_____

List a small goal that you will work towards accomplishing tomorrow:

_____

_____

_____

_____

_____

Date: ___/___/___

How are you feeling today? (Angry/*Depressed/Happy/Indifferent/Sick*)

_____

_____

_____

_____

_____

_____

Did you receive a Hoover from the Narcissist today? If yes, how did you respond?

_____

_____

_____

_____

_____

List a small goal that you will work towards accomplishing tomorrow:

_____

_____

_____

_____

_____

_____

Date: ___/___/___

How are you feeling today? (Angry/*Depressed/Happy/Indifferent/Sick*)

_____

_____

_____

_____

_____

_____

_____

Did you receive a Hoover from the Narcissist today? If yes, how did you respond?

_____

_____

_____

_____

_____

_____

List a small goal that you will work towards accomplishing tomorrow:

_____

_____

_____

_____

_____

_____

Date: ___/___/___

How are you feeling today? (Angry/*Depressed/Happy/Indifferent/Sick*)

_____

_____

_____

_____

_____

_____

_____

Did you receive a Hoover from the Narcissist today? If yes, how did you respond?

_____

_____

_____

_____

_____

_____

List a small goal that you will work towards accomplishing tomorrow:

_____

_____

_____

_____

_____

_____

Date: ___/___/___

How are you feeling today? (Angry/*Depressed*/*Happy*/*Indifferent*/*Sick*)

_____

_____

_____

_____

_____

_____

Did you receive a Hoover from the Narcissist today? If yes, how did you respond?

_____

_____

_____

_____

_____

List a small goal that you will work towards accomplishing tomorrow:

_____

_____

_____

_____

_____

Date: ___/___/___

How are you feeling today? (Angry/*Depressed/Happy/Indifferent/Sick*)

_____

_____

_____

_____

_____

_____

_____

Did you receive a Hoover from the Narcissist today? If yes, how did you respond?

_____

_____

_____

_____

_____

_____

List a small goal that you will work towards accomplishing tomorrow:

_____

_____

_____

_____

_____

_____

Date: ___/___/___

How are you feeling today? (Angry/*Depressed/Happy/Indifferent/Sick*)

_____

_____

_____

_____

_____

_____

Did you receive a Hoover from the Narcissist today? If yes, how did you respond?

_____

_____

_____

_____

_____

List a small goal that you will work towards accomplishing tomorrow:

_____

_____

_____

_____

_____

Date: ___/___/___

How are you feeling today? (Angry/*Depressed*/*Happy*/*Indifferent*/*Sick*)

_____

_____

_____

_____

_____

_____

_____

Did you receive a Hoover from the Narcissist today? If yes, how did you respond?

_____

_____

_____

_____

_____

_____

List a small goal that you will work towards accomplishing tomorrow:

_____

_____

_____

_____

_____

_____

Date: ___/___/___

How are you feeling today? (Angry/*Depressed/Happy/Indifferent/Sick*)

_____

_____

_____

_____

_____

_____

Did you receive a Hoover from the Narcissist today? If yes, how did you respond?

_____

_____

_____

_____

_____

List a small goal that you will work towards accomplishing tomorrow:

_____

_____

_____

_____

_____

_____

Date: ___/___/___

How are you feeling today? (Angry/*Depressed*/*Happy*/*Indifferent*/*Sick*)

_____

_____

_____

_____

_____

_____

_____

Did you receive a Hoover from the Narcissist today? If yes, how did you respond?

_____

_____

_____

_____

_____

List a small goal that you will work towards accomplishing tomorrow:

_____

_____

_____

_____

_____

_____

Date: ___/___/___

How are you feeling today? (Angry/*Depressed/Happy/Indifferent/Sick*)

_____

_____

_____

_____

_____

_____

Did you receive a Hoover from the Narcissist today? If yes, how did you respond?

_____

_____

_____

_____

List a small goal that you will work towards accomplishing tomorrow:

_____

_____

_____

_____

_____

Date: ___/___/___

How are you feeling today? (Angry/*Depressed*/*Happy*/*Indifferent*/*Sick*)

_____

_____

_____

_____

_____

_____

_____

Did you receive a Hoover from the Narcissist today? If yes, how did you respond?

_____

_____

_____

_____

_____

_____

List a small goal that you will work towards accomplishing tomorrow:

_____

_____

_____

_____

_____

_____

Date: ___/___/___

How are you feeling today? (Angry/*Depressed/Happy/Indifferent/Sick*)

_____

_____

_____

_____

_____

_____

Did you receive a Hoover from the Narcissist today? If yes, how did you respond?

_____

_____

_____

_____

_____

List a small goal that you will work towards accomplishing tomorrow:

_____

_____

_____

_____

_____

_____

Date: ___/___/___

How are you feeling today? (Angry/*Depressed*/*Happy*/*Indifferent*/*Sick*)

_____

_____

_____

_____

_____

_____

_____

Did you receive a Hoover from the Narcissist today? If yes, how did you respond?

_____

_____

_____

_____

_____

_____

List a small goal that you will work towards accomplishing tomorrow:

_____

_____

_____

_____

_____

_____

Date: ___/___/___

How are you feeling today? (Angry/*Depressed/Happy/Indifferent/Sick*)

_____

_____

_____

_____

_____

_____

_____

Did you receive a Hoover from the Narcissist today? If yes, how did you respond?

_____

_____

_____

_____

_____

List a small goal that you will work towards accomplishing tomorrow:

_____

_____

_____

_____

_____

Date: ___/___/___

How are you feeling today? (Angry/*Depressed/Happy/Indifferent/Sick*)

_____

_____

_____

_____

_____

_____

Did you receive a Hoover from the Narcissist today? If yes, how did you respond?

_____

_____

_____

_____

_____

List a small goal that you will work towards accomplishing tomorrow:

_____

_____

_____

_____

_____

Date: ___/___/___

How are you feeling today? (Angry/*Depressed/Happy/Indifferent/Sick*)

_____

_____

_____

_____

_____

_____

_____

Did you receive a Hoover from the Narcissist today? If yes, how did you respond?

_____

_____

_____

_____

_____

_____

List a small goal that you will work towards accomplishing tomorrow:

_____

_____

_____

_____

_____

_____

"Don't lose your present to your past."
-Unknown

"Sometimes it takes a good fall to know where you really stand."
-*Hayley Williams*

Date: ___/___/___

How are you feeling today? (Angry/*Depressed/Happy/Indifferent/Sick*)

_____

_____

_____

_____

_____

_____

_____

Did you receive a Hoover from the Narcissist today? If yes, how did you respond?

_____

_____

_____

_____

_____

_____

List a small goal that you will work towards accomplishing tomorrow:

_____

_____

_____

_____

_____

_____

Date: ___/___/___

How are you feeling today? (Angry/*Depressed/Happy/Indifferent/Sick*)

_____
_____
_____
_____
_____
_____
_____

Did you receive a Hoover from the Narcissist today? If yes, how did you respond?

_____
_____
_____
_____
_____
_____

List a small goal that you will work towards accomplishing tomorrow:

_____
_____
_____
_____
_____
_____

Date: ___/___/___

How are you feeling today? (Angry/*Depressed*/*Happy*/*Indifferent*/*Sick*)

_____

_____

_____

_____

_____

_____

_____

Did you receive a Hoover from the Narcissist today? If yes, how did you respond?

_____

_____

_____

_____

_____

_____

List a small goal that you will work towards accomplishing tomorrow:

_____

_____

_____

_____

_____

_____

Date: ___/___/___

How are you feeling today? (Angry/*Depressed*/*Happy*/*Indifferent*/*Sick*)

_____

_____

_____

_____

_____

_____

_____

Did you receive a Hoover from the Narcissist today? If yes, how did you respond?

_____

_____

_____

_____

_____

_____

List a small goal that you will work towards accomplishing tomorrow:

_____

_____

_____

_____

_____

_____

Date: ___/___/___

How are you feeling today? (Angry/*Depressed/Happy/Indifferent/Sick*)

_____

_____

_____

_____

_____

_____

_____

Did you receive a Hoover from the Narcissist today? If yes, how did you respond?

_____

_____

_____

_____

_____

_____

List a small goal that you will work towards accomplishing tomorrow:

_____

_____

_____

_____

_____

_____

Date: ___/___/___

How are you feeling today? (Angry/*Depressed*/*Happy*/*Indifferent*/*Sick*)

_____

_____

_____

_____

_____

_____

Did you receive a Hoover from the Narcissist today? If yes, how did you respond?

_____

_____

_____

_____

_____

List a small goal that you will work towards accomplishing tomorrow:

_____

_____

_____

_____

_____

Date: ___/___/___

How are you feeling today? (Angry/*Depressed/Happy/Indifferent/Sick*)

_____

_____

_____

_____

_____

_____

_____

Did you receive a Hoover from the Narcissist today? If yes, how did you respond?

_____

_____

_____

_____

_____

_____

List a small goal that you will work towards accomplishing tomorrow:

_____

_____

_____

_____

_____

_____

Date: ___/___/___

How are you feeling today? (Angry/*Depressed/Happy/Indifferent/Sick*)

_____

_____

_____

_____

_____

_____

_____

Did you receive a Hoover from the Narcissist today? If yes, how did you respond?

_____

_____

_____

_____

_____

_____

List a small goal that you will work towards accomplishing tomorrow:

_____

_____

_____

_____

_____

_____

Date: ___/___/___

How are you feeling today? (Angry/*Depressed*/*Happy*/*Indifferent*/*Sick*)

_____

_____

_____

_____

_____

_____

_____

Did you receive a Hoover from the Narcissist today? If yes, how did you respond?

_____

_____

_____

_____

_____

_____

List a small goal that you will work towards accomplishing tomorrow:

_____

_____

_____

_____

_____

_____

Date: ___/___/___

How are you feeling today? (Angry/*Depressed/Happy/Indifferent/Sick*)

_____

_____

_____

_____

_____

_____

Did you receive a Hoover from the Narcissist today? If yes, how did you respond?

_____

_____

_____

_____

_____

List a small goal that you will work towards accomplishing tomorrow:

_____

_____

_____

_____

_____

Date: ___/___/___

How are you feeling today? (Angry/*Depressed*/*Happy*/*Indifferent*/*Sick*)

_____

_____

_____

_____

_____

_____

Did you receive a Hoover from the Narcissist today? If yes, how did you respond?

_____

_____

_____

_____

_____

List a small goal that you will work towards accomplishing tomorrow:

_____

_____

_____

_____

_____

_____

Date: ___/___/___

How are you feeling today? (Angry/*Depressed/Happy/Indifferent/Sick*)

_____

_____

_____

_____

_____

_____

Did you receive a Hoover from the Narcissist today? If yes, how did you respond?

_____

_____

_____

_____

_____

List a small goal that you will work towards accomplishing tomorrow:

_____

_____

_____

_____

_____

Date: ___/___/___

How are you feeling today? (Angry/*Depressed*/*Happy*/*Indifferent*/*Sick*)

_____

_____

_____

_____

_____

_____

Did you receive a Hoover from the Narcissist today? If yes, how did you respond?

_____

_____

_____

_____

_____

List a small goal that you will work towards accomplishing tomorrow:

_____

_____

_____

_____

_____

_____

Date: ___/___/___

How are you feeling today? (Angry/*Depressed/Happy/Indifferent/Sick*)

_____
_____
_____
_____
_____
_____
_____

Did you receive a Hoover from the Narcissist today? If yes, how did you respond?

_____
_____
_____
_____
_____
_____

List a small goal that you will work towards accomplishing tomorrow:

_____
_____
_____
_____
_____
_____

Date: ___/___/___

How are you feeling today? (Angry/*Depressed/Happy/Indifferent/Sick*)

_____

_____

_____

_____

_____

_____

_____

Did you receive a Hoover from the Narcissist today? If yes, how did you respond?

_____

_____

_____

_____

_____

_____

List a small goal that you will work towards accomplishing tomorrow:

_____

_____

_____

_____

_____

_____

Date: ___/___/___

How are you feeling today? (Angry/*Depressed/Happy/Indifferent/Sick*)

_____

_____

_____

_____

_____

_____

_____

Did you receive a Hoover from the Narcissist today? If yes, how did you respond?

_____

_____

_____

_____

_____

_____

List a small goal that you will work towards accomplishing tomorrow:

_____

_____

_____

_____

_____

_____

Date: ___/___/___

How are you feeling today? (Angry/*Depressed/Happy/Indifferent/Sick*)

_____

_____

_____

_____

_____

_____

_____

Did you receive a Hoover from the Narcissist today? If yes, how did you respond?

_____

_____

_____

_____

_____

_____

List a small goal that you will work towards accomplishing tomorrow:

_____

_____

_____

_____

_____

_____

Date: ___/___/___

How are you feeling today? (Angry/*Depressed*/*Happy*/*Indifferent*/*Sick*)

_____

_____

_____

_____

_____

_____

_____

Did you receive a Hoover from the Narcissist today? If yes, how did you respond?

_____

_____

_____

_____

_____

List a small goal that you will work towards accomplishing tomorrow:

_____

_____

_____

_____

_____

_____

Date: ___/___/___

How are you feeling today? (Angry/*Depressed/Happy/Indifferent/Sick*)

_____

_____

_____

_____

_____

_____

_____

Did you receive a Hoover from the Narcissist today? If yes, how did you respond?

_____

_____

_____

_____

_____

_____

List a small goal that you will work towards accomplishing tomorrow:

_____

_____

_____

_____

_____

_____

_____

Date: ___/___/___

How are you feeling today? (Angry/*Depressed*/*Happy*/*Indifferent*/*Sick*)

_____

_____

_____

_____

_____

_____

Did you receive a Hoover from the Narcissist today? If yes, how did you respond?

_____

_____

_____

_____

_____

List a small goal that you will work towards accomplishing tomorrow:

_____

_____

_____

_____

_____

Date: ___/___/___

How are you feeling today? (Angry/*Depressed*/*Happy*/*Indifferent*/*Sick*)

_____

_____

_____

_____

_____

_____

Did you receive a Hoover from the Narcissist today? If yes, how did you respond?

_____

_____

_____

_____

_____

List a small goal that you will work towards accomplishing tomorrow:

_____

_____

_____

_____

_____

Date: ___/___/___

How are you feeling today? (Angry/*Depressed*/*Happy*/*Indifferent*/*Sick*)

_____

_____

_____

_____

_____

_____

_____

Did you receive a Hoover from the Narcissist today? If yes, how did you respond?

_____

_____

_____

_____

_____

List a small goal that you will work towards accomplishing tomorrow:

_____

_____

_____

_____

_____

Date: ___/___/___

How are you feeling today? (Angry/*Depressed*/*Happy*/*Indifferent*/*Sick*)

_____

_____

_____

_____

_____

_____

Did you receive a Hoover from the Narcissist today? If yes, how did you respond?

_____

_____

_____

_____

_____

List a small goal that you will work towards accomplishing tomorrow:

_____

_____

_____

_____

_____

_____

Date: ___/___/___

How are you feeling today? (Angry/*Depressed/Happy/Indifferent/Sick*)

_____

_____

_____

_____

_____

_____

_____

Did you receive a Hoover from the Narcissist today? If yes, how did you respond?

_____

_____

_____

_____

_____

_____

List a small goal that you will work towards accomplishing tomorrow:

_____

_____

_____

_____

_____

_____

Date: ___/___/___

How are you feeling today? (Angry/*Depressed/Happy/Indifferent/Sick*)

_____

_____

_____

_____

_____

_____

_____

Did you receive a Hoover from the Narcissist today? If yes, how did you respond?

_____

_____

_____

_____

_____

_____

List a small goal that you will work towards accomplishing tomorrow:

_____

_____

_____

_____

_____

_____

Date: ___/___/___

How are you feeling today? (Angry/*Depressed*/*Happy*/*Indifferent*/*Sick*)

_____

_____

_____

_____

_____

_____

Did you receive a Hoover from the Narcissist today? If yes, how did you respond?

_____

_____

_____

_____

_____

List a small goal that you will work towards accomplishing tomorrow:

_____

_____

_____

_____

_____

Date: ___/___/___

How are you feeling today? (Angry/*Depressed/Happy/Indifferent/Sick*)

_____

_____

_____

_____

_____

_____

_____

Did you receive a Hoover from the Narcissist today? If yes, how did you respond?

_____

_____

_____

_____

_____

_____

List a small goal that you will work towards accomplishing tomorrow:

_____

_____

_____

_____

_____

_____

Date: ___/___/___

How are you feeling today? (Angry/*Depressed/Happy/Indifferent/Sick*)

_____

_____

_____

_____

_____

_____

_____

Did you receive a Hoover from the Narcissist today? If yes, how did you respond?

_____

_____

_____

_____

_____

List a small goal that you will work towards accomplishing tomorrow:

_____

_____

_____

_____

_____

_____

Date: ___/___/___

How are you feeling today? (Angry/*Depressed*/*Happy*/*Indifferent*/*Sick*)

_____

_____

_____

_____

_____

_____

Did you receive a Hoover from the Narcissist today? If yes, how did you respond?

_____

_____

_____

_____

_____

_____

List a small goal that you will work towards accomplishing tomorrow:

_____

_____

_____

_____

_____

_____

Date: ___/___/___

How are you feeling today? (Angry/*Depressed*/*Happy*/*Indifferent*/*Sick*)

_____

_____

_____

_____

_____

_____

Did you receive a Hoover from the Narcissist today? If yes, how did you respond?

_____

_____

_____

_____

_____

List a small goal that you will work towards accomplishing tomorrow:

_____

_____

_____

_____

_____

_____

Date: ___/___/___

How are you feeling today? (Angry/*Depressed*/*Happy*/*Indifferent*/*Sick*)

_____

_____

_____

_____

_____

_____

Did you receive a Hoover from the Narcissist today? If yes, how did you respond?

_____

_____

_____

_____

_____

List a small goal that you will work towards accomplishing tomorrow:

_____

_____

_____

_____

_____

Date: ___/___/___

How are you feeling today? (Angry/*Depressed/Happy/Indifferent/Sick*)

_____

_____

_____

_____

_____

_____

_____

Did you receive a Hoover from the Narcissist today? If yes, how did you respond?

_____

_____

_____

_____

_____

List a small goal that you will work towards accomplishing tomorrow:

_____

_____

_____

_____

_____

_____

Date: ___/___/___

How are you feeling today? (Angry/*Depressed/Happy/Indifferent/Sick*)

_____

_____

_____

_____

_____

_____

_____

Did you receive a Hoover from the Narcissist today? If yes, how did you respond?

_____

_____

_____

_____

_____

_____

List a small goal that you will work towards accomplishing tomorrow:

_____

_____

_____

_____

_____

_____

Date: ___/___/___

How are you feeling today? (Angry/*Depressed/Happy/Indifferent/Sick*)

_____

_____

_____

_____

_____

_____

Did you receive a Hoover from the Narcissist today? If yes, how did you respond?

_____

_____

_____

_____

_____

List a small goal that you will work towards accomplishing tomorrow:

_____

_____

_____

_____

_____

_____

"Though he may stumble, he will not fall, for the LORD upholds him with his hand."

-Psalm 37:24

"I can do all things through Christ which strengthen me."
—Phillippians 4:13

Date: ___/___/___

How are you feeling today? (Angry/*Depressed/Happy/Indifferent/Sick*)

_____

_____

_____

_____

_____

_____

Did you receive a Hoover from the Narcissist today? If yes, how did you respond?

_____

_____

_____

_____

_____

_____

List a small goal that you will work towards accomplishing tomorrow:

_____

_____

_____

_____

_____

_____

Date: ___/___/___

How are you feeling today? (Angry/*Depressed/Happy/Indifferent/Sick*)

_____

_____

_____

_____

_____

_____

_____

Did you receive a Hoover from the Narcissist today? If yes, how did you respond?

_____

_____

_____

_____

_____

List a small goal that you will work towards accomplishing tomorrow:

_____

_____

_____

_____

_____

Date: ___/___/___

How are you feeling today? (Angry/*Depressed/Happy/Indifferent/Sick*)

_____

_____

_____

_____

_____

_____

_____

Did you receive a Hoover from the Narcissist today? If yes, how did you respond?

_____

_____

_____

_____

_____

_____

List a small goal that you will work towards accomplishing tomorrow:

_____

_____

_____

_____

_____

_____

Date: ___/___/___

How are you feeling today? (Angry/*Depressed*/*Happy*/*Indifferent*/*Sick*)

_____

_____

_____

_____

_____

_____

Did you receive a Hoover from the Narcissist today? If yes, how did you respond?

_____

_____

_____

_____

_____

List a small goal that you will work towards accomplishing tomorrow:

_____

_____

_____

_____

_____

Date: ___/___/___

How are you feeling today? (Angry/*Depressed/Happy/Indifferent/Sick*)

_____

_____

_____

_____

_____

_____

_____

Did you receive a Hoover from the Narcissist today? If yes, how did you respond?

_____

_____

_____

_____

_____

_____

List a small goal that you will work towards accomplishing tomorrow:

_____

_____

_____

_____

_____

_____

Date: ___/___/___

How are you feeling today? (Angry/*Depressed/Happy/Indifferent/Sick*)

_____

_____

_____

_____

_____

_____

_____

Did you receive a Hoover from the Narcissist today? If yes, how did you respond?

_____

_____

_____

_____

_____

List a small goal that you will work towards accomplishing tomorrow:

_____

_____

_____

_____

_____

Date: ___/___/___

How are you feeling today? (Angry/*Depressed/Happy/Indifferent/Sick*)

_____

_____

_____

_____

_____

_____

_____

Did you receive a Hoover from the Narcissist today? If yes, how did you respond?

_____

_____

_____

_____

_____

_____

List a small goal that you will work towards accomplishing tomorrow:

_____

_____

_____

_____

_____

_____

Date: ___/___/___

How are you feeling today? (Angry/*Depressed/Happy/Indifferent/Sick*)

_____

_____

_____

_____

_____

_____

Did you receive a Hoover from the Narcissist today? If yes, how did you respond?

_____

_____

_____

_____

_____

List a small goal that you will work towards accomplishing tomorrow:

_____

_____

_____

_____

_____

Date: ___/___/___

How are you feeling today? (Angry/*Depressed/Happy/Indifferent/Sick*)

_____

_____

_____

_____

_____

_____

Did you receive a Hoover from the Narcissist today? If yes, how did you respond?

_____

_____

_____

_____

_____

List a small goal that you will work towards accomplishing tomorrow:

_____

_____

_____

_____

_____

_____

Date: ___/___/___

How are you feeling today? (Angry/*Depressed*/*Happy*/*Indifferent*/*Sick*)

_____

_____

_____

_____

_____

_____

_____

Did you receive a Hoover from the Narcissist today? If yes, how did you respond?

_____

_____

_____

_____

_____

_____

List a small goal that you will work towards accomplishing tomorrow:

_____

_____

_____

_____

_____

_____

Date: ___/___/___

How are you feeling today? (Angry/*Depressed/Happy/Indifferent/Sick*)

_____

_____

_____

_____

_____

_____

_____

Did you receive a Hoover from the Narcissist today? If yes, how did you respond?

_____

_____

_____

_____

_____

_____

List a small goal that you will work towards accomplishing tomorrow:

_____

_____

_____

_____

_____

_____

Date: ___/___/___

How are you feeling today? (Angry/*Depressed/Happy/Indifferent/Sick*)

_____

_____

_____

_____

_____

_____

Did you receive a Hoover from the Narcissist today? If yes, how did you respond?

_____

_____

_____

_____

_____

List a small goal that you will work towards accomplishing tomorrow:

_____

_____

_____

_____

_____

Date: ___/___/___

How are you feeling today? (Angry/*Depressed/Happy/Indifferent/Sick*)

_____

_____

_____

_____

_____

_____

_____

Did you receive a Hoover from the Narcissist today? If yes, how did you respond?

_____

_____

_____

_____

_____

_____

List a small goal that you will work towards accomplishing tomorrow:

_____

_____

_____

_____

_____

_____

Date: ___/___/___

How are you feeling today? (Angry/*Depressed/Happy/Indifferent/Sick*)

_____

_____

_____

_____

_____

_____

Did you receive a Hoover from the Narcissist today? If yes, how did you respond?

_____

_____

_____

_____

_____

List a small goal that you will work towards accomplishing tomorrow:

_____

_____

_____

_____

_____

Date: ___/___/___

How are you feeling today? (Angry/*Depressed/Happy/Indifferent/Sick*)

_____

_____

_____

_____

_____

_____

_____

Did you receive a Hoover from the Narcissist today? If yes, how did you respond?

_____

_____

_____

_____

_____

_____

List a small goal that you will work towards accomplishing tomorrow:

_____

_____

_____

_____

_____

_____

Date: ___/___/___

How are you feeling today? (Angry/*Depressed/Happy/Indifferent/Sick*)

_____

_____

_____

_____

_____

_____

Did you receive a Hoover from the Narcissist today? If yes, how did you respond?

_____

_____

_____

_____

_____

_____

List a small goal that you will work towards accomplishing tomorrow:

_____

_____

_____

_____

_____

_____

Date: ___/___/___

How are you feeling today? (Angry/*Depressed/Happy/Indifferent/Sick*)

_____

_____

_____

_____

_____

_____

_____

Did you receive a Hoover from the Narcissist today? If yes, how did you respond?

_____

_____

_____

_____

_____

_____

List a small goal that you will work towards accomplishing tomorrow:

_____

_____

_____

_____

_____

_____

_____

Date: ___/___/___

How are you feeling today? (Angry/*Depressed/Happy/Indifferent/Sick*)

_____

_____

_____

_____

_____

_____

_____

Did you receive a Hoover from the Narcissist today? If yes, how did you respond?

_____

_____

_____

_____

_____

_____

List a small goal that you will work towards accomplishing tomorrow:

_____

_____

_____

_____

_____

_____

Date: ___/___/___

How are you feeling today? (Angry/*Depressed*/Happy/*Indifferent*/*Sick*)

_____

_____

_____

_____

_____

_____

Did you receive a Hoover from the Narcissist today? If yes, how did you respond?

_____

_____

_____

_____

_____

List a small goal that you will work towards accomplishing tomorrow:

_____

_____

_____

_____

_____

_____

Date: ___/___/___

How are you feeling today? (Angry/*Depressed/Happy/Indifferent/Sick*)

_____

_____

_____

_____

_____

_____

Did you receive a Hoover from the Narcissist today? If yes, how did you respond?

_____

_____

_____

_____

_____

List a small goal that you will work towards accomplishing tomorrow:

_____

_____

_____

_____

_____

Date: ___/___/___

How are you feeling today? (Angry/*Depressed*/*Happy*/*Indifferent*/*Sick*)

_____

_____

_____

_____

_____

_____

_____

Did you receive a Hoover from the Narcissist today? If yes, how did you respond?

_____

_____

_____

_____

_____

_____

List a small goal that you will work towards accomplishing tomorrow:

_____

_____

_____

_____

_____

_____

Date: ___/___/___

How are you feeling today? (Angry/*Depressed*/*Happy*/*Indifferent*/*Sick*)

_____

_____

_____

_____

_____

_____

_____

Did you receive a Hoover from the Narcissist today? If yes, how did you respond?

_____

_____

_____

_____

_____

List a small goal that you will work towards accomplishing tomorrow:

_____

_____

_____

_____

_____

_____

Date: ___/___/___

How are you feeling today? (Angry/*Depressed/Happy/Indifferent/Sick*)

_____

_____

_____

_____

_____

_____

_____

Did you receive a Hoover from the Narcissist today? If yes, how did you respond?

_____

_____

_____

_____

_____

_____

List a small goal that you will work towards accomplishing tomorrow:

_____

_____

_____

_____

_____

_____

Date: ___/___/___

How are you feeling today? (Angry/*Depressed/Happy/Indifferent/Sick*)

_____

_____

_____

_____

_____

_____

Did you receive a Hoover from the Narcissist today? If yes, how did you respond?

_____

_____

_____

_____

_____

List a small goal that you will work towards accomplishing tomorrow:

_____

_____

_____

_____

_____

Date: ___/___/___

How are you feeling today? (Angry/*Depressed*/*Happy*/*Indifferent*/*Sick*)

_____

_____

_____

_____

_____

_____

_____

Did you receive a Hoover from the Narcissist today? If yes, how did you respond?

_____

_____

_____

_____

_____

List a small goal that you will work towards accomplishing tomorrow:

_____

_____

_____

_____

_____

Date: ___/___/___

How are you feeling today? (Angry/*Depressed/Happy/Indifferent/Sick*)

_____

_____

_____

_____

_____

_____

_____

Did you receive a Hoover from the Narcissist today? If yes, how did you respond?

_____

_____

_____

_____

_____

List a small goal that you will work towards accomplishing tomorrow:

_____

_____

_____

_____

_____

_____

Date: ___/___/___

How are you feeling today? (Angry/*Depressed*/*Happy*/*Indifferent*/*Sick*)

_____
_____
_____
_____
_____
_____
_____

Did you receive a Hoover from the Narcissist today? If yes, how did you respond?

_____
_____
_____
_____
_____
_____

List a small goal that you will work towards accomplishing tomorrow:

_____
_____
_____
_____
_____
_____

Date: ___/___/___

How are you feeling today? (Angry/*Depressed/Happy/Indifferent/Sick*)

_____

_____

_____

_____

_____

_____

Did you receive a Hoover from the Narcissist today? If yes, how did you respond?

_____

_____

_____

_____

_____

List a small goal that you will work towards accomplishing tomorrow:

_____

_____

_____

_____

_____

"Everything you can imagine is real."
-*Pablo Picasso*

"Success is falling nine times and getting up ten."
-Jon Bon Jovi

Date: ___/___/___

How are you feeling today? (Angry/*Depressed*/*Happy*/*Indifferent*/*Sick*)

_____

_____

_____

_____

_____

_____

_____

Did you receive a Hoover from the Narcissist today? If yes, how did you respond?

_____

_____

_____

_____

_____

_____

List a small goal that you will work towards accomplishing tomorrow:

_____

_____

_____

_____

_____

_____

Date: ___/___/___

How are you feeling today? (Angry/*Depressed/Happy/Indifferent/Sick*)

_____

_____

_____

_____

_____

_____

_____

Did you receive a Hoover from the Narcissist today? If yes, how did you respond?

_____

_____

_____

_____

_____

List a small goal that you will work towards accomplishing tomorrow:

_____

_____

_____

_____

_____

Date: ___/___/___

How are you feeling today? (Angry/*Depressed/Happy/Indifferent/Sick*)

_____

_____

_____

_____

_____

_____

Did you receive a Hoover from the Narcissist today? If yes, how did you respond?

_____

_____

_____

_____

_____

List a small goal that you will work towards accomplishing tomorrow:

_____

_____

_____

_____

_____

Date: ___/___/___

How are you feeling today? (Angry/*Depressed/Happy/Indifferent/Sick*)

_____

_____

_____

_____

_____

_____

Did you receive a Hoover from the Narcissist today? If yes, how did you respond?

_____

_____

_____

_____

List a small goal that you will work towards accomplishing tomorrow:

_____

_____

_____

_____

_____

Date: ___/___/___

How are you feeling today? (Angry/*Depressed/Happy/Indifferent/Sick*)

_____

_____

_____

_____

_____

_____

Did you receive a Hoover from the Narcissist today? If yes, how did you respond?

_____

_____

_____

_____

_____

List a small goal that you will work towards accomplishing tomorrow:

_____

_____

_____

_____

_____

Date: ___/___/___

How are you feeling today? (Angry/*Depressed*/*Happy*/*Indifferent*/*Sick*)

_____

_____

_____

_____

_____

_____

_____

Did you receive a Hoover from the Narcissist today? If yes, how did you respond?

_____

_____

_____

_____

_____

List a small goal that you will work towards accomplishing tomorrow:

_____

_____

_____

_____

_____

_____

Date: ___/___/___

How are you feeling today? (Angry/*Depressed/Happy/Indifferent/Sick*)

_____

_____

_____

_____

_____

_____

_____

Did you receive a Hoover from the Narcissist today? If yes, how did you respond?

_____

_____

_____

_____

_____

_____

List a small goal that you will work towards accomplishing tomorrow:

_____

_____

_____

_____

_____

_____

Date: ___/___/___

How are you feeling today? (Angry/*Depressed/Happy/Indifferent/Sick*)

_____

_____

_____

_____

_____

_____

Did you receive a Hoover from the Narcissist today? If yes, how did you respond?

_____

_____

_____

_____

_____

List a small goal that you will work towards accomplishing tomorrow:

_____

_____

_____

_____

_____

_____

Date: ___/___/___

How are you feeling today? (Angry/*Depressed*/*Happy*/*Indifferent*/*Sick*)

_____

_____

_____

_____

_____

_____

Did you receive a Hoover from the Narcissist today? If yes, how did you respond?

_____

_____

_____

_____

_____

List a small goal that you will work towards accomplishing tomorrow:

_____

_____

_____

_____

_____

_____

Date: ___/___/___

How are you feeling today? (Angry/*Depressed*/*Happy*/*Indifferent*/*Sick*)

_____

_____

_____

_____

_____

_____

Did you receive a Hoover from the Narcissist today? If yes, how did you respond?

_____

_____

_____

_____

_____

List a small goal that you will work towards accomplishing tomorrow:

_____

_____

_____

_____

_____

_____

Date: ___/___/___

How are you feeling today? (Angry/*Depressed/Happy/Indifferent/Sick*)

_____

_____

_____

_____

_____

_____

_____

Did you receive a Hoover from the Narcissist today? If yes, how did you respond?

_____

_____

_____

_____

_____

_____

List a small goal that you will work towards accomplishing tomorrow:

_____

_____

_____

_____

_____

_____

Date: ___/___/___

How are you feeling today? (Angry/*Depressed/Happy/Indifferent/Sick*)

_____

_____

_____

_____

_____

_____

_____

Did you receive a Hoover from the Narcissist today? If yes, how did you respond?

_____

_____

_____

_____

_____

_____

List a small goal that you will work towards accomplishing tomorrow:

_____

_____

_____

_____

_____

_____

Date: ___/___/___

How are you feeling today? (Angry/*Depressed*/Happy/*Indifferent*/*Sick*)

_____

_____

_____

_____

_____

_____

Did you receive a Hoover from the Narcissist today? If yes, how did you respond?

_____

_____

_____

_____

_____

List a small goal that you will work towards accomplishing tomorrow:

_____

_____

_____

_____

_____

_____

Date: ___/___/___

How are you feeling today? (Angry/*Depressed*/*Happy*/*Indifferent*/*Sick*)

_____

_____

_____

_____

_____

Did you receive a Hoover from the Narcissist today? If yes, how did you respond?

_____

_____

_____

_____

List a small goal that you will work towards accomplishing tomorrow:

_____

_____

_____

_____

_____

Date: ___/___/___

How are you feeling today? (Angry/*Depressed*/*Happy*/*Indifferent*/*Sick*)

_____

_____

_____

_____

_____

_____

_____

Did you receive a Hoover from the Narcissist today? If yes, how did you respond?

_____

_____

_____

_____

_____

List a small goal that you will work towards accomplishing tomorrow:

_____

_____

_____

_____

_____

_____

Date: ___/___/___

How are you feeling today? (Angry/*Depressed/Happy/Indifferent/Sick*)

_____

_____

_____

_____

_____

_____

Did you receive a Hoover from the Narcissist today? If yes, how did you respond?

_____

_____

_____

_____

_____

List a small goal that you will work towards accomplishing tomorrow:

_____

_____

_____

_____

_____

Date: ___/___/___

How are you feeling today? (Angry/*Depressed/Happy/Indifferent/Sick*)

_____

_____

_____

_____

_____

_____

_____

Did you receive a Hoover from the Narcissist today? If yes, how did you respond?

_____

_____

_____

_____

_____

_____

List a small goal that you will work towards accomplishing tomorrow:

_____

_____

_____

_____

_____

_____

Date: ___/___/___

How are you feeling today? (Angry/*Depressed*/*Happy*/*Indifferent*/*Sick*)

_____

_____

_____

_____

_____

_____

Did you receive a Hoover from the Narcissist today? If yes, how did you respond?

_____

_____

_____

_____

_____

List a small goal that you will work towards accomplishing tomorrow:

_____

_____

_____

_____

_____

Date: ___/___/___

How are you feeling today? (Angry/*Depressed*/*Happy*/*Indifferent*/*Sick*)

_____

_____

_____

_____

_____

_____

_____

Did you receive a Hoover from the Narcissist today? If yes, how did you respond?

_____

_____

_____

_____

_____

_____

List a small goal that you will work towards accomplishing tomorrow:

_____

_____

_____

_____

_____

_____

_____

Date: ___/___/___

How are you feeling today? (Angry/*Depressed/Happy/Indifferent/Sick*)

_____

_____

_____

_____

_____

_____

Did you receive a Hoover from the Narcissist today? If yes, how did you respond?

_____

_____

_____

_____

List a small goal that you will work towards accomplishing tomorrow:

_____

_____

_____

_____

_____

Date: ___/___/___

How are you feeling today? (Angry/*Depressed/Happy/Indifferent/Sick*)

_____

_____

_____

_____

_____

_____

_____

Did you receive a Hoover from the Narcissist today? If yes, how did you respond?

_____

_____

_____

_____

_____

_____

List a small goal that you will work towards accomplishing tomorrow:

_____

_____

_____

_____

_____

_____

Date: ___/___/___

How are you feeling today? (Angry/*Depressed/Happy/Indifferent/Sick*)

_____

_____

_____

_____

_____

_____

_____

Did you receive a Hoover from the Narcissist today? If yes, how did you respond?

_____

_____

_____

_____

_____

_____

List a small goal that you will work towards accomplishing tomorrow:

_____

_____

_____

_____

_____

_____

"Every mistake just adds to your story."
-*Unknown*

"It's up to you."
-Unknown

Date: ___/___/___

How are you feeling today? (Angry/*Depressed/Happy/Indifferent/Sick*)

_____

_____

_____

_____

_____

_____

Did you receive a Hoover from the Narcissist today? If yes, how did you respond?

_____

_____

_____

_____

_____

_____

List a small goal that you will work towards accomplishing tomorrow:

_____

_____

_____

_____

_____

_____

Date: ___/___/___

How are you feeling today? (Angry/*Depressed/Happy/Indifferent/Sick*)

_____

_____

_____

_____

_____

_____

_____

Did you receive a Hoover from the Narcissist today? If yes, how did you respond?

_____

_____

_____

_____

_____

_____

List a small goal that you will work towards accomplishing tomorrow:

_____

_____

_____

_____

_____

_____

Date: ___/___/___

How are you feeling today? (Angry/*Depressed/Happy/Indifferent/Sick*)

_____

_____

_____

_____

_____

_____

_____

Did you receive a Hoover from the Narcissist today? If yes, how did you respond?

_____

_____

_____

_____

_____

_____

List a small goal that you will work towards accomplishing tomorrow:

_____

_____

_____

_____

_____

_____

_____

Date: ___/___/___

How are you feeling today? (Angry/*Depressed/Happy/Indifferent/Sick*)

_____

_____

_____

_____

_____

_____

Did you receive a Hoover from the Narcissist today? If yes, how did you respond?

_____

_____

_____

_____

_____

List a small goal that you will work towards accomplishing tomorrow:

_____

_____

_____

_____

_____

Date: ___/___/___

How are you feeling today? (Angry/*Depressed*/*Happy*/*Indifferent*/*Sick*)

_____

_____

_____

_____

_____

_____

_____

Did you receive a Hoover from the Narcissist today? If yes, how did you respond?

_____

_____

_____

_____

_____

List a small goal that you will work towards accomplishing tomorrow:

_____

_____

_____

_____

_____

_____

Date: ___/___/___

How are you feeling today? (Angry/*Depressed*/*Happy*/*Indifferent*/*Sick*)

_____

_____

_____

_____

_____

_____

Did you receive a Hoover from the Narcissist today? If yes, how did you respond?

_____

_____

_____

_____

_____

List a small goal that you will work towards accomplishing tomorrow:

_____

_____

_____

_____

_____

Date: ___/___/___

How are you feeling today? (Angry/*Depressed/Happy/Indifferent/Sick*)

_____

_____

_____

_____

_____

_____

Did you receive a Hoover from the Narcissist today? If yes, how did you respond?

_____

_____

_____

_____

_____

List a small goal that you will work towards accomplishing tomorrow:

_____

_____

_____

_____

_____

Date: ___/___/___

How are you feeling today? (Angry/*Depressed/Happy/Indifferent/Sick*)

_____

_____

_____

_____

_____

_____

_____

Did you receive a Hoover from the Narcissist today? If yes, how did you respond?

_____

_____

_____

_____

_____

List a small goal that you will work towards accomplishing tomorrow:

_____

_____

_____

_____

_____

Date: ___/___/___

How are you feeling today? (Angry/*Depressed/Happy/Indifferent/Sick*)

_____

_____

_____

_____

_____

_____

Did you receive a Hoover from the Narcissist today? If yes, how did you respond?

_____

_____

_____

_____

_____

List a small goal that you will work towards accomplishing tomorrow:

_____

_____

_____

_____

_____

Date: ___/___/___

How are you feeling today? (Angry/*Depressed*/*Happy*/*Indifferent*/*Sick*)

_____

_____

_____

_____

_____

_____

_____

Did you receive a Hoover from the Narcissist today? If yes, how did you respond?

_____

_____

_____

_____

_____

List a small goal that you will work towards accomplishing tomorrow:

_____

_____

_____

_____

_____

_____

Date: ___/___/___

How are you feeling today? (Angry/*Depressed*/*Happy*/*Indifferent*/*Sick*)

_____

_____

_____

_____

_____

_____

_____

Did you receive a Hoover from the Narcissist today? If yes, how did you respond?

_____

_____

_____

_____

_____

_____

List a small goal that you will work towards accomplishing tomorrow:

_____

_____

_____

_____

_____

_____

Date: ___/___/___

How are you feeling today? (Angry/*Depressed/Happy/Indifferent/Sick*)

_____

_____

_____

_____

_____

_____

_____

Did you receive a Hoover from the Narcissist today? If yes, how did you respond?

_____

_____

_____

_____

_____

List a small goal that you will work towards accomplishing tomorrow:

_____

_____

_____

_____

_____

_____

Date: ___/___/___

How are you feeling today? (Angry/*Depressed*/*Happy*/*Indifferent*/*Sick*)

_____

_____

_____

_____

_____

_____

Did you receive a Hoover from the Narcissist today? If yes, how did you respond?

_____

_____

_____

_____

_____

List a small goal that you will work towards accomplishing tomorrow:

_____

_____

_____

_____

_____

_____

Date: ___/___/___

How are you feeling today? (Angry/*Depressed/Happy/Indifferent/Sick*)

_____

_____

_____

_____

_____

_____

_____

Did you receive a Hoover from the Narcissist today? If yes, how did you respond?

_____

_____

_____

_____

_____

List a small goal that you will work towards accomplishing tomorrow:

_____

_____

_____

_____

_____

_____

Date: ___/___/___

How are you feeling today? (Angry/*Depressed*/*Happy*/*Indifferent*/*Sick*)

_____

_____

_____

_____

_____

_____

_____

Did you receive a Hoover from the Narcissist today? If yes, how did you respond?

_____

_____

_____

_____

_____

List a small goal that you will work towards accomplishing tomorrow:

_____

_____

_____

_____

_____

_____

Date: ___/___/___

How are you feeling today? (Angry/*Depressed/Happy/Indifferent/Sick*)

_____

_____

_____

_____

_____

_____

Did you receive a Hoover from the Narcissist today? If yes, how did you respond?

_____

_____

_____

_____

List a small goal that you will work towards accomplishing tomorrow:

_____

_____

_____

_____

_____

Date: ___/___/___

How are you feeling today? (Angry/*Depressed*/*Happy*/*Indifferent*/*Sick*)

_____

_____

_____

_____

_____

_____

Did you receive a Hoover from the Narcissist today? If yes, how did you respond?

_____

_____

_____

_____

_____

List a small goal that you will work towards accomplishing tomorrow:

_____

_____

_____

_____

_____

_____

Date: ___/___/___

How are you feeling today? (Angry/*Depressed/Happy/Indifferent/Sick*)

_____

_____

_____

_____

_____

_____

Did you receive a Hoover from the Narcissist today? If yes, how did you respond?

_____

_____

_____

_____

_____

List a small goal that you will work towards accomplishing tomorrow:

_____

_____

_____

_____

_____

Date: ___/___/___

How are you feeling today? (Angry/*Depressed*/*Happy*/*Indifferent*/*Sick*)

_____

_____

_____

_____

_____

_____

Did you receive a Hoover from the Narcissist today? If yes, how did you respond?

_____

_____

_____

_____

_____

List a small goal that you will work towards accomplishing tomorrow:

_____

_____

_____

_____

_____

_____

Date: ___/___/___

How are you feeling today? (Angry/*Depressed*/*Happy*/*Indifferent*/*Sick*)

_____

_____

_____

_____

_____

_____

_____

Did you receive a Hoover from the Narcissist today? If yes, how did you respond?

_____

_____

_____

_____

_____

List a small goal that you will work towards accomplishing tomorrow:

_____

_____

_____

_____

_____

Date: ___/___/___

How are you feeling today? (Angry/*Depressed/Happy/Indifferent/Sick*)

_____

_____

_____

_____

_____

_____

_____

Did you receive a Hoover from the Narcissist today? If yes, how did you respond?

_____

_____

_____

_____

_____

List a small goal that you will work towards accomplishing tomorrow:

_____

_____

_____

_____

_____

_____

Date: ___/___/___

How are you feeling today? (Angry/*Depressed/Happy/Indifferent/Sick*)

_____

_____

_____

_____

_____

_____

Did you receive a Hoover from the Narcissist today? If yes, how did you respond?

_____

_____

_____

_____

_____

List a small goal that you will work towards accomplishing tomorrow:

_____

_____

_____

_____

_____

_____

Date: ___/___/___

How are you feeling today? (Angry/*Depressed/Happy/Indifferent/Sick*)

_____

_____

_____

_____

_____

_____

_____

Did you receive a Hoover from the Narcissist today? If yes, how did you respond?

_____

_____

_____

_____

_____

_____

List a small goal that you will work towards accomplishing tomorrow:

_____

_____

_____

_____

_____

_____

Date: ___/___/___

How are you feeling today? (Angry/*Depressed/Happy/Indifferent/Sick*)

_____

_____

_____

_____

_____

_____

Did you receive a Hoover from the Narcissist today? If yes, how did you respond?

_____

_____

_____

_____

_____

List a small goal that you will work towards accomplishing tomorrow:

_____

_____

_____

_____

_____

Date: ___/___/___

How are you feeling today? (Angry/*Depressed/Happy/Indifferent/Sick*)

_____

_____

_____

_____

_____

_____

Did you receive a Hoover from the Narcissist today? If yes, how did you respond?

_____

_____

_____

_____

_____

List a small goal that you will work towards accomplishing tomorrow:

_____

_____

_____

_____

_____

Date: ___/___/___

How are you feeling today? (Angry/*Depressed/Happy/Indifferent/Sick*)

_____

_____

_____

_____

_____

_____

Did you receive a Hoover from the Narcissist today? If yes, how did you respond?

_____

_____

_____

_____

_____

List a small goal that you will work towards accomplishing tomorrow:

_____

_____

_____

_____

_____

Date: ___/___/___

How are you feeling today? (Angry/*Depressed*/*Happy*/*Indifferent*/*Sick*)

_____

_____

_____

_____

_____

_____

Did you receive a Hoover from the Narcissist today? If yes, how did you respond?

_____

_____

_____

_____

_____

List a small goal that you will work towards accomplishing tomorrow:

_____

_____

_____

_____

_____

Date: ___/___/___

How are you feeling today? (Angry/*Depressed/Happy/Indifferent/Sick*)

_____
_____
_____
_____
_____
_____
_____

Did you receive a Hoover from the Narcissist today? If yes, how did you respond?

_____
_____
_____
_____
_____

List a small goal that you will work towards accomplishing tomorrow:

_____
_____
_____
_____
_____
_____

Date: ___/___/___

How are you feeling today? (Angry/*Depressed/Happy/Indifferent/Sick*)

_____

_____

_____

_____

_____

_____

_____

Did you receive a Hoover from the Narcissist today? If yes, how did you respond?

_____

_____

_____

_____

_____

_____

List a small goal that you will work towards accomplishing tomorrow:

_____

_____

_____

_____

_____

_____

Date: ___/___/___

How are you feeling today? (Angry/*Depressed/Happy/Indifferent/Sick*)

_____

_____

_____

_____

_____

_____

Did you receive a Hoover from the Narcissist today? If yes, how did you respond?

_____

_____

_____

_____

_____

List a small goal that you will work towards accomplishing tomorrow:

_____

_____

_____

_____

_____

Date: ___/___/___

How are you feeling today? (Angry/*Depressed/Happy/Indifferent/Sick*)

_____

_____

_____

_____

_____

_____

Did you receive a Hoover from the Narcissist today? If yes, how did you respond?

_____

_____

_____

_____

_____

List a small goal that you will work towards accomplishing tomorrow:

_____

_____

_____

_____

_____

Date: ___/___/___

How are you feeling today? (Angry/*Depressed*/*Happy*/*Indifferent*/*Sick*)

_____

_____

_____

_____

_____

_____

_____

Did you receive a Hoover from the Narcissist today? If yes, how did you respond?

_____

_____

_____

_____

_____

List a small goal that you will work towards accomplishing tomorrow:

_____

_____

_____

_____

_____

Date: ___/___/___

How are you feeling today? (Angry/*Depressed/Happy/Indifferent/Sick*)

_____

_____

_____

_____

_____

_____

_____

Did you receive a Hoover from the Narcissist today? If yes, how did you respond?

_____

_____

_____

_____

_____

_____

List a small goal that you will work towards accomplishing tomorrow:

_____

_____

_____

_____

_____

_____

Date: ___/___/___

How are you feeling today? (Angry/*Depressed/Happy/Indifferent/Sick*)

_____

_____

_____

_____

_____

_____

_____

Did you receive a Hoover from the Narcissist today? If yes, how did you respond?

_____

_____

_____

_____

_____

List a small goal that you will work towards accomplishing tomorrow:

_____

_____

_____

_____

_____

_____

Date: ___/___/___

How are you feeling today? (Angry/*Depressed*/*Happy*/*Indifferent*/*Sick*)

_____

_____

_____

_____

_____

_____

Did you receive a Hoover from the Narcissist today? If yes, how did you respond?

_____

_____

_____

_____

_____

List a small goal that you will work towards accomplishing tomorrow:

_____

_____

_____

_____

_____

_____

Date: ___/___/___

How are you feeling today? (Angry/*Depressed/Happy/Indifferent/Sick*)

_____

_____

_____

_____

_____

_____

Did you receive a Hoover from the Narcissist today? If yes, how did you respond?

_____

_____

_____

_____

_____

List a small goal that you will work towards accomplishing tomorrow:

_____

_____

_____

_____

_____

Date: ___/___/___

How are you feeling today? (Angry/*Depressed*/*Happy*/*Indifferent*/*Sick*)

_____

_____

_____

_____

_____

_____

Did you receive a Hoover from the Narcissist today? If yes, how did you respond?

_____

_____

_____

_____

_____

List a small goal that you will work towards accomplishing tomorrow:

_____

_____

_____

_____

_____

Date: ___/___/___

How are you feeling today? (Angry/*Depressed/Happy/Indifferent/Sick*)

_____

_____

_____

_____

_____

_____

_____

Did you receive a Hoover from the Narcissist today? If yes, how did you respond?

_____

_____

_____

_____

_____

List a small goal that you will work towards accomplishing tomorrow:

_____

_____

_____

_____

_____

_____

Date: ___/___/___

How are you feeling today? (Angry/*Depressed*/*Happy*/*Indifferent*/*Sick*)

_____

_____

_____

_____

_____

_____

Did you receive a Hoover from the Narcissist today? If yes, how did you respond?

_____

_____

_____

_____

_____

List a small goal that you will work towards accomplishing tomorrow:

_____

_____

_____

_____

_____

Date: ___/___/___

How are you feeling today? (Angry/*Depressed/Happy/Indifferent/Sick*)

_____

_____

_____

_____

_____

_____

_____

Did you receive a Hoover from the Narcissist today? If yes, how did you respond?

_____

_____

_____

_____

_____

List a small goal that you will work towards accomplishing tomorrow:

_____

_____

_____

_____

_____

"Trust in the Lord with all thine heart; and lean not unto thine own understanding. In all thy ways acknowledge him, and he shall direct thy paths."

-Proverbs 3:5-6

"Cast your cares on the Lord
and he will sustain you;

He will never let the righteous
be shaken."

-Psalm 55:22

Date: ___/___/___

How are you feeling today? (Angry/*Depressed*/*Happy*/*Indifferent*/*Sick*)

_____

_____

_____

_____

_____

_____

_____

Did you receive a Hoover from the Narcissist today? If yes, how did you respond?

_____

_____

_____

_____

_____

_____

List a small goal that you will work towards accomplishing tomorrow:

_____

_____

_____

_____

_____

_____

Date: ___/___/___

How are you feeling today? (Angry/*Depressed/Happy/Indifferent/Sick*)

_____

_____

_____

_____

_____

_____

Did you receive a Hoover from the Narcissist today? If yes, how did you respond?

_____

_____

_____

_____

_____

List a small goal that you will work towards accomplishing tomorrow:

_____

_____

_____

_____

_____

_____

Date: ___/___/___

How are you feeling today? (Angry/*Depressed*/*Happy*/*Indifferent*/*Sick*)

_____

_____

_____

_____

_____

_____

Did you receive a Hoover from the Narcissist today? If yes, how did you respond?

_____

_____

_____

_____

_____

List a small goal that you will work towards accomplishing tomorrow:

_____

_____

_____

_____

_____

Date: ___/___/___

How are you feeling today? (Angry/*Depressed*/*Happy*/*Indifferent*/*Sick*)

_____

_____

_____

_____

_____

_____

Did you receive a Hoover from the Narcissist today? If yes, how did you respond?

_____

_____

_____

_____

List a small goal that you will work towards accomplishing tomorrow:

_____

_____

_____

_____

_____

Date: ___/___/___

How are you feeling today? (Angry/*Depressed*/*Happy*/*Indifferent*/*Sick*)

_____

_____

_____

_____

_____

_____

Did you receive a Hoover from the Narcissist today? If yes, how did you respond?

_____

_____

_____

_____

_____

List a small goal that you will work towards accomplishing tomorrow:

_____

_____

_____

_____

_____

_____

Date: ___/___/___

How are you feeling today? (Angry/*Depressed*/*Happy*/*Indifferent*/*Sick*)

_____

_____

_____

_____

_____

_____

Did you receive a Hoover from the Narcissist today? If yes, how did you respond?

_____

_____

_____

_____

_____

List a small goal that you will work towards accomplishing tomorrow:

_____

_____

_____

_____

_____

Date: ___/___/___

How are you feeling today? (Angry/*Depressed/Happy/Indifferent/Sick*)

_____

_____

_____

_____

_____

_____

Did you receive a Hoover from the Narcissist today? If yes, how did you respond?

_____

_____

_____

_____

_____

List a small goal that you will work towards accomplishing tomorrow:

_____

_____

_____

_____

_____

Date: ___/___/___

How are you feeling today? (Angry/*Depressed/Happy/Indifferent/Sick*)

_____
_____
_____
_____
_____
_____
_____

Did you receive a Hoover from the Narcissist today? If yes, how did you respond?

_____
_____
_____
_____
_____
_____

List a small goal that you will work towards accomplishing tomorrow:

_____
_____
_____
_____
_____
_____

Date: ___/___/___

How are you feeling today? (Angry/*Depressed*/*Happy*/*Indifferent*/*Sick*)

_____

_____

_____

_____

_____

_____

Did you receive a Hoover from the Narcissist today? If yes, how did you respond?

_____

_____

_____

_____

_____

List a small goal that you will work towards accomplishing tomorrow:

_____

_____

_____

_____

_____

_____

Date: ___/___/___

How are you feeling today? (Angry/*Depressed*/*Happy*/*Indifferent*/*Sick*)

_____

_____

_____

_____

_____

_____

Did you receive a Hoover from the Narcissist today? If yes, how did you respond?

_____

_____

_____

_____

_____

List a small goal that you will work towards accomplishing tomorrow:

_____

_____

_____

_____

_____

Date: ___/___/___

How are you feeling today? (Angry/*Depressed/Happy/Indifferent/Sick*)

_____

_____

_____

_____

_____

_____

Did you receive a Hoover from the Narcissist today? If yes, how did you respond?

_____

_____

_____

_____

_____

_____

List a small goal that you will work towards accomplishing tomorrow:

_____

_____

_____

_____

_____

_____

Date: ___/___/___

How are you feeling today? (Angry/*Depressed*/*Happy*/*Indifferent*/*Sick*)

_____

_____

_____

_____

_____

_____

Did you receive a Hoover from the Narcissist today? If yes, how did you respond?

_____

_____

_____

_____

_____

List a small goal that you will work towards accomplishing tomorrow:

_____

_____

_____

_____

_____

Date: ___/___/___

How are you feeling today? (Angry/*Depressed*/*Happy*/*Indifferent*/*Sick*)

_____

_____

_____

_____

_____

_____

_____

Did you receive a Hoover from the Narcissist today? If yes, how did you respond?

_____

_____

_____

_____

_____

_____

List a small goal that you will work towards accomplishing tomorrow:

_____

_____

_____

_____

_____

_____

Date: ___/___/___

How are you feeling today? (Angry/*Depressed/Happy/Indifferent/Sick*)

_____

_____

_____

_____

_____

_____

Did you receive a Hoover from the Narcissist today? If yes, how did you respond?

_____

_____

_____

_____

_____

List a small goal that you will work towards accomplishing tomorrow:

_____

_____

_____

_____

_____

Date: ___/___/___

How are you feeling today? (Angry/*Depressed/Happy/Indifferent/Sick*)

_____

_____

_____

_____

_____

_____

Did you receive a Hoover from the Narcissist today? If yes, how did you respond?

_____

_____

_____

_____

_____

List a small goal that you will work towards accomplishing tomorrow:

_____

_____

_____

_____

_____

Date: ___/___/___

How are you feeling today? (Angry/*Depressed/Happy/Indifferent/Sick*)

_____

_____

_____

_____

_____

_____

Did you receive a Hoover from the Narcissist today? If yes, how did you respond?

_____

_____

_____

_____

_____

List a small goal that you will work towards accomplishing tomorrow:

_____

_____

_____

_____

_____

Date: ___/___/___

How are you feeling today? (Angry/*Depressed*/*Happy*/*Indifferent*/*Sick*)

_____

_____

_____

_____

_____

_____

Did you receive a Hoover from the Narcissist today? If yes, how did you respond?

_____

_____

_____

_____

_____

List a small goal that you will work towards accomplishing tomorrow:

_____

_____

_____

_____

_____

_____

Date: ___/___/___

How are you feeling today? (Angry/*Depressed/Happy/Indifferent/Sick*)

_____
_____
_____
_____
_____
_____
_____

Did you receive a Hoover from the Narcissist today? If yes, how did you respond?

_____
_____
_____
_____
_____
_____

List a small goal that you will work towards accomplishing tomorrow:

_____
_____
_____
_____
_____
_____

Date: ___/___/___

How are you feeling today? (Angry/*Depressed*/*Happy*/*Indifferent*/*Sick*)

_____

_____

_____

_____

_____

_____

Did you receive a Hoover from the Narcissist today? If yes, how did you respond?

_____

_____

_____

_____

_____

List a small goal that you will work towards accomplishing tomorrow:

_____

_____

_____

_____

_____

_____

Date: ___/___/___

How are you feeling today? (Angry/*Depressed/Happy/Indifferent/Sick*)

_____

_____

_____

_____

_____

_____

Did you receive a Hoover from the Narcissist today? If yes, how did you respond?

_____

_____

_____

_____

_____

List a small goal that you will work towards accomplishing tomorrow:

_____

_____

_____

_____

_____

_____

Date: ___/___/___

How are you feeling today? (Angry/*Depressed*/*Happy*/*Indifferent*/*Sick*)

_____

_____

_____

_____

_____

_____

Did you receive a Hoover from the Narcissist today? If yes, how did you respond?

_____

_____

_____

_____

_____

List a small goal that you will work towards accomplishing tomorrow:

_____

_____

_____

_____

_____

Date: ___/___/___

How are you feeling today? (Angry/*Depressed*/*Happy*/*Indifferent*/*Sick*)

_____

_____

_____

_____

_____

_____

Did you receive a Hoover from the Narcissist today? If yes, how did you respond?

_____

_____

_____

_____

_____

List a small goal that you will work towards accomplishing tomorrow:

_____

_____

_____

_____

_____

_____

Date: ___/___/___

How are you feeling today? (Angry/*Depressed/Happy/Indifferent/Sick*)

_____

_____

_____

_____

_____

_____

_____

Did you receive a Hoover from the Narcissist today? If yes, how did you respond?

_____

_____

_____

_____

_____

_____

List a small goal that you will work towards accomplishing tomorrow:

_____

_____

_____

_____

_____

_____

Date: ___/___/___

How are you feeling today? (Angry/*Depressed*/*Happy*/*Indifferent*/*Sick*)

_____

_____

_____

_____

_____

_____

Did you receive a Hoover from the Narcissist today? If yes, how did you respond?

_____

_____

_____

_____

_____

List a small goal that you will work towards accomplishing tomorrow:

_____

_____

_____

_____

_____

Date: ___/___/___

How are you feeling today? (Angry/*Depressed*/*Happy*/*Indifferent*/*Sick*)

_____

_____

_____

_____

_____

_____

Did you receive a Hoover from the Narcissist today? If yes, how did you respond?

_____

_____

_____

_____

_____

List a small goal that you will work towards accomplishing tomorrow:

_____

_____

_____

_____

_____

_____

Date: ___/___/___

How are you feeling today? (Angry/*Depressed/Happy/Indifferent/Sick*)

_____

_____

_____

_____

_____

_____

_____

Did you receive a Hoover from the Narcissist today? If yes, how did you respond?

_____

_____

_____

_____

_____

_____

List a small goal that you will work towards accomplishing tomorrow:

_____

_____

_____

_____

_____

_____

Date: ___/___/___

How are you feeling today? (Angry/*Depressed/Happy/Indifferent/Sick*)

_____

_____

_____

_____

_____

_____

Did you receive a Hoover from the Narcissist today? If yes, how did you respond?

_____

_____

_____

_____

_____

List a small goal that you will work towards accomplishing tomorrow:

_____

_____

_____

_____

_____

Date: ___/___/___

How are you feeling today? (Angry/*Depressed*/*Happy*/*Indifferent*/*Sick*)

_____

_____

_____

_____

_____

_____

_____

Did you receive a Hoover from the Narcissist today? If yes, how did you respond?

_____

_____

_____

_____

_____

List a small goal that you will work towards accomplishing tomorrow:

_____

_____

_____

_____

_____

Date: ___/___/___

How are you feeling today? (Angry/*Depressed/Happy/Indifferent/Sick*)

_____

_____

_____

_____

_____

_____

_____

Did you receive a Hoover from the Narcissist today? If yes, how did you respond?

_____

_____

_____

_____

_____

_____

List a small goal that you will work towards accomplishing tomorrow:

_____

_____

_____

_____

_____

_____

Date: ___/___/___

How are you feeling today? (Angry/*Depressed/Happy/Indifferent/Sick*)

_____
_____
_____
_____
_____
_____

Did you receive a Hoover from the Narcissist today? If yes, how did you respond?

_____
_____
_____
_____
_____

List a small goal that you will work towards accomplishing tomorrow:

_____
_____
_____
_____
_____

Date: ___/___/___

How are you feeling today? (Angry/*Depressed/Happy/Indifferent/Sick*)

_____

_____

_____

_____

_____

_____

Did you receive a Hoover from the Narcissist today? If yes, how did you respond?

_____

_____

_____

_____

_____

List a small goal that you will work towards accomplishing tomorrow:

_____

_____

_____

_____

_____

Date: ___/___/___

How are you feeling today? (Angry/*Depressed/Happy/Indifferent/Sick*)

_____

_____

_____

_____

_____

_____

Did you receive a Hoover from the Narcissist today? If yes, how did you respond?

_____

_____

_____

_____

_____

List a small goal that you will work towards accomplishing tomorrow:

_____

_____

_____

_____

_____

Date: ___/___/___

How are you feeling today? (Angry/*Depressed*/*Happy*/*Indifferent*/*Sick*)

_____

_____

_____

_____

_____

_____

Did you receive a Hoover from the Narcissist today? If yes, how did you respond?

_____

_____

_____

_____

_____

List a small goal that you will work towards accomplishing tomorrow:

_____

_____

_____

_____

_____

_____

Date: ___/___/___

How are you feeling today? (Angry/*Depressed*/*Happy*/*Indifferent*/*Sick*)

_____

_____

_____

_____

_____

_____

_____

Did you receive a Hoover from the Narcissist today? If yes, how did you respond?

_____

_____

_____

_____

_____

_____

List a small goal that you will work towards accomplishing tomorrow:

_____

_____

_____

_____

_____

_____

"Be joyful in hope, patient in affliction, faithful in prayer."
-Romans 12:12

"God is not unjust; he will not forget your work and the love you have shown him as you have helped his people and continue to help them."
-Hebrews 6:10

Date: ___/___/___

How are you feeling today? (Angry/*Depressed*/*Happy*/*Indifferent*/*Sick*)

_____

_____

_____

_____

_____

_____

_____

Did you receive a Hoover from the Narcissist today? If yes, how did you respond?

_____

_____

_____

_____

_____

_____

List a small goal that you will work towards accomplishing tomorrow:

_____

_____

_____

_____

_____

_____

Date: ___/___/___

How are you feeling today? (Angry/*Depressed/Happy/Indifferent/Sick*)

_____
_____
_____
_____
_____
_____
_____

Did you receive a Hoover from the Narcissist today? If yes, how did you respond?

_____
_____
_____
_____
_____

List a small goal that you will work towards accomplishing tomorrow:

_____
_____
_____
_____
_____
_____

Date: ___/___/___

How are you feeling today? (Angry/*Depressed/Happy/Indifferent/Sick*)

_____

_____

_____

_____

_____

_____

_____

Did you receive a Hoover from the Narcissist today? If yes, how did you respond?

_____

_____

_____

_____

_____

List a small goal that you will work towards accomplishing tomorrow:

_____

_____

_____

_____

_____

_____

Date: ___/___/___

How are you feeling today? (Angry/*Depressed/Happy/Indifferent/Sick*)

_____

_____

_____

_____

_____

_____

_____

Did you receive a Hoover from the Narcissist today? If yes, how did you respond?

_____

_____

_____

_____

_____

List a small goal that you will work towards accomplishing tomorrow:

_____

_____

_____

_____

_____

Date: ___/___/___

How are you feeling today? (Angry/*Depressed*/*Happy*/*Indifferent*/*Sick*)

_____
_____
_____
_____
_____
_____
_____

Did you receive a Hoover from the Narcissist today? If yes, how did you respond?

_____
_____
_____
_____
_____
_____

List a small goal that you will work towards accomplishing tomorrow:

_____
_____
_____
_____
_____
_____

Date: ___/___/___

How are you feeling today? (Angry/*Depressed*/*Happy*/*Indifferent*/*Sick*)

_____

_____

_____

_____

_____

_____

_____

Did you receive a Hoover from the Narcissist today? If yes, how did you respond?

_____

_____

_____

_____

_____

List a small goal that you will work towards accomplishing tomorrow:

_____

_____

_____

_____

_____

_____

Date: ___/___/___

How are you feeling today? (Angry/*Depressed/Happy/Indifferent/Sick*)

_____

_____

_____

_____

_____

_____

Did you receive a Hoover from the Narcissist today? If yes, how did you respond?

_____

_____

_____

_____

_____

List a small goal that you will work towards accomplishing tomorrow:

_____

_____

_____

_____

_____

Date: ___/___/___

How are you feeling today? (Angry/*Depressed/Happy/Indifferent/Sick*)

_____

_____

_____

_____

_____

_____

_____

Did you receive a Hoover from the Narcissist today? If yes, how did you respond?

_____

_____

_____

_____

_____

List a small goal that you will work towards accomplishing tomorrow:

_____

_____

_____

_____

_____

_____

Date: ___/___/___

How are you feeling today? (Angry/*Depressed*/*Happy*/*Indifferent*/*Sick*)

_____

_____

_____

_____

_____

_____

Did you receive a Hoover from the Narcissist today? If yes, how did you respond?

_____

_____

_____

_____

_____

List a small goal that you will work towards accomplishing tomorrow:

_____

_____

_____

_____

_____

Date: ___/___/___

How are you feeling today? (Angry/*Depressed/Happy/Indifferent/Sick*)

_____

_____

_____

_____

_____

_____

_____

Did you receive a Hoover from the Narcissist today? If yes, how did you respond?

_____

_____

_____

_____

_____

_____

List a small goal that you will work towards accomplishing tomorrow:

_____

_____

_____

_____

_____

_____

Date: ___/___/___

How are you feeling today? (Angry/*Depressed/Happy/Indifferent/Sick*)

_____

_____

_____

_____

_____

_____

_____

Did you receive a Hoover from the Narcissist today? If yes, how did you respond?

_____

_____

_____

_____

_____

List a small goal that you will work towards accomplishing tomorrow:

_____

_____

_____

_____

_____

Date: ___/___/___

How are you feeling today? (Angry/*Depressed*/*Happy*/*Indifferent*/*Sick*)

_____

_____

_____

_____

_____

_____

_____

Did you receive a Hoover from the Narcissist today? If yes, how did you respond?

_____

_____

_____

_____

_____

List a small goal that you will work towards accomplishing tomorrow:

_____

_____

_____

_____

_____

Date: ___/___/___

How are you feeling today? (Angry/*Depressed*/*Happy*/*Indifferent*/*Sick*)

_____

_____

_____

_____

_____

_____

Did you receive a Hoover from the Narcissist today? If yes, how did you respond?

_____

_____

_____

_____

_____

List a small goal that you will work towards accomplishing tomorrow:

_____

_____

_____

_____

_____

Date: ___/___/___

How are you feeling today? (Angry/*Depressed/Happy/Indifferent/Sick*)

_____

_____

_____

_____

_____

_____

_____

Did you receive a Hoover from the Narcissist today? If yes, how did you respond?

_____

_____

_____

_____

_____

List a small goal that you will work towards accomplishing tomorrow:

_____

_____

_____

_____

_____

Date: ___/___/___

How are you feeling today? (Angry/*Depressed/Happy/Indifferent/Sick*)

_____

_____

_____

_____

_____

_____

Did you receive a Hoover from the Narcissist today? If yes, how did you respond?

_____

_____

_____

_____

_____

List a small goal that you will work towards accomplishing tomorrow:

_____

_____

_____

_____

_____

Date: ___/___/___

How are you feeling today? (Angry/*Depressed*/*Happy*/*Indifferent*/*Sick*)

_____

_____

_____

_____

_____

_____

_____

Did you receive a Hoover from the Narcissist today? If yes, how did you respond?

_____

_____

_____

_____

_____

List a small goal that you will work towards accomplishing tomorrow:

_____

_____

_____

_____

_____

"Erase the word 'failure' from your vocabulary."
-Mary Lou Retton

"Champions keep playing until they get it right."
-Billie Jean King

Date: ___/___/___

How are you feeling today? (Angry/*Depressed*/*Happy*/*Indifferent*/*Sick*)

_____

_____

_____

_____

_____

_____

Did you receive a Hoover from the Narcissist today? If yes, how did you respond?

_____

_____

_____

_____

_____

List a small goal that you will work towards accomplishing tomorrow:

_____

_____

_____

_____

_____

Date: ___/___/___

How are you feeling today? (Angry/*Depressed*/*Happy*/*Indifferent*/*Sick*)

_____

_____

_____

_____

_____

_____

Did you receive a Hoover from the Narcissist today? If yes, how did you respond?

_____

_____

_____

_____

_____

_____

List a small goal that you will work towards accomplishing tomorrow:

_____

_____

_____

_____

_____

_____

Date: ___/___/___

How are you feeling today? (Angry/*Depressed*/Happy/*Indifferent*/*Sick*)

_____

_____

_____

_____

_____

_____

Did you receive a Hoover from the Narcissist today? If yes, how did you respond?

_____

_____

_____

_____

_____

List a small goal that you will work towards accomplishing tomorrow:

_____

_____

_____

_____

_____

_____

Date: ___/___/___

How are you feeling today? (Angry/*Depressed*/*Happy*/*Indifferent*/*Sick*)

_____

_____

_____

_____

_____

_____

Did you receive a Hoover from the Narcissist today? If yes, how did you respond?

_____

_____

_____

_____

_____

List a small goal that you will work towards accomplishing tomorrow:

_____

_____

_____

_____

_____

_____

Date: ___/___/___

How are you feeling today? (Angry/*Depressed/Happy/Indifferent/Sick*)

_____

_____

_____

_____

_____

_____

Did you receive a Hoover from the Narcissist today? If yes, how did you respond?

_____

_____

_____

_____

_____

List a small goal that you will work towards accomplishing tomorrow:

_____

_____

_____

_____

_____

_____

Date: ___/___/___

How are you feeling today? (Angry/*Depressed/Happy/Indifferent/Sick*)

Did you receive a Hoover from the Narcissist today? If yes, how did you respond?

List a small goal that you will work towards accomplishing tomorrow:

Date: ___/___/___

How are you feeling today? (Angry/*Depressed*/*Happy*/*Indifferent*/*Sick*)

_____

_____

_____

_____

_____

_____

Did you receive a Hoover from the Narcissist today? If yes, how did you respond?

_____

_____

_____

_____

_____

List a small goal that you will work towards accomplishing tomorrow:

_____

_____

_____

_____

_____

Date: ___/___/___

How are you feeling today? (Angry/*Depressed/Happy/Indifferent/Sick*)

_____
_____
_____
_____
_____
_____
_____

Did you receive a Hoover from the Narcissist today? If yes, how did you respond?

_____
_____
_____
_____
_____
_____

List a small goal that you will work towards accomplishing tomorrow:

_____
_____
_____
_____
_____
_____

Date: ___/___/___

How are you feeling today? (Angry/*Depressed/Happy/Indifferent/Sick*)

_____

_____

_____

_____

_____

_____

Did you receive a Hoover from the Narcissist today? If yes, how did you respond?

_____

_____

_____

_____

_____

List a small goal that you will work towards accomplishing tomorrow:

_____

_____

_____

_____

_____

Date: ___/___/___

How are you feeling today? (Angry/*Depressed*/*Happy*/*Indifferent*/*Sick*)

_____

_____

_____

_____

_____

_____

Did you receive a Hoover from the Narcissist today? If yes, how did you respond?

_____

_____

_____

_____

_____

List a small goal that you will work towards accomplishing tomorrow:

_____

_____

_____

_____

_____

Date: ___/___/___

How are you feeling today? (Angry/*Depressed/Happy/Indifferent/Sick*)

_____

_____

_____

_____

_____

_____

_____

Did you receive a Hoover from the Narcissist today? If yes, how did you respond?

_____

_____

_____

_____

_____

List a small goal that you will work towards accomplishing tomorrow:

_____

_____

_____

_____

_____

Date: ___/___/___

How are you feeling today? (Angry/*Depressed/Happy/Indifferent/Sick*)

_____

_____

_____

_____

_____

_____

_____

Did you receive a Hoover from the Narcissist today? If yes, how did you respond?

_____

_____

_____

_____

_____

_____

List a small goal that you will work towards accomplishing tomorrow:

_____

_____

_____

_____

_____

_____

Date: ___/___/___

How are you feeling today? (Angry/*Depressed/Happy/Indifferent/Sick*)

_____

_____

_____

_____

_____

_____

Did you receive a Hoover from the Narcissist today? If yes, how did you respond?

_____

_____

_____

_____

_____

List a small goal that you will work towards accomplishing tomorrow:

_____

_____

_____

_____

_____

Date: ___/___/___

How are you feeling today? (Angry/*Depressed*/*Happy*/*Indifferent*/*Sick*)

_____

_____

_____

_____

_____

_____

Did you receive a Hoover from the Narcissist today? If yes, how did you respond?

_____

_____

_____

_____

_____

List a small goal that you will work towards accomplishing tomorrow:

_____

_____

_____

_____

_____

Date: ___/___/___

How are you feeling today? (Angry/*Depressed*/*Happy*/*Indifferent*/*Sick*)

_____

_____

_____

_____

_____

_____

_____

Did you receive a Hoover from the Narcissist today? If yes, how did you respond?

_____

_____

_____

_____

_____

_____

List a small goal that you will work towards accomplishing tomorrow:

_____

_____

_____

_____

_____

_____

Date: ___/___/___

How are you feeling today? (Angry/*Depressed*/*Happy*/*Indifferent*/*Sick*)

_____

_____

_____

_____

_____

_____

_____

Did you receive a Hoover from the Narcissist today? If yes, how did you respond?

_____

_____

_____

_____

_____

List a small goal that you will work towards accomplishing tomorrow:

_____

_____

_____

_____

_____

_____

Date: ___/___/___

How are you feeling today? (Angry/*Depressed*/*Happy*/*Indifferent*/*Sick*)

_____

_____

_____

_____

_____

_____

Did you receive a Hoover from the Narcissist today? If yes, how did you respond?

_____

_____

_____

_____

_____

List a small goal that you will work towards accomplishing tomorrow:

_____

_____

_____

_____

_____

_____

Date: ___/___/___

How are you feeling today? (Angry/*Depressed/Happy/Indifferent/Sick*)

_____

_____

_____

_____

_____

_____

_____

Did you receive a Hoover from the Narcissist today? If yes, how did you respond?

_____

_____

_____

_____

_____

List a small goal that you will work towards accomplishing tomorrow:

_____

_____

_____

_____

_____

_____

Date: ___/___/___

How are you feeling today? (Angry/*Depressed/Happy/Indifferent/Sick*)

_____

_____

_____

_____

_____

_____

_____

Did you receive a Hoover from the Narcissist today? If yes, how did you respond?

_____

_____

_____

_____

_____

_____

List a small goal that you will work towards accomplishing tomorrow:

_____

_____

_____

_____

_____

_____

Date: ___/___/___

How are you feeling today? (Angry/*Depressed/Happy/Indifferent/Sick*)

_____

_____

_____

_____

_____

_____

_____

Did you receive a Hoover from the Narcissist today? If yes, how did you respond?

_____

_____

_____

_____

_____

List a small goal that you will work towards accomplishing tomorrow:

_____

_____

_____

_____

_____

Date: ___/___/___

How are you feeling today? (Angry/*Depressed*/*Happy*/*Indifferent*/*Sick*)

_____

_____

_____

_____

_____

_____

_____

Did you receive a Hoover from the Narcissist today? If yes, how did you respond?

_____

_____

_____

_____

_____

_____

List a small goal that you will work towards accomplishing tomorrow:

_____

_____

_____

_____

_____

_____

Date: ___/___/___

How are you feeling today? (Angry/*Depressed*/*Happy*/*Indifferent*/*Sick*)

_____

_____

_____

_____

_____

_____

_____

Did you receive a Hoover from the Narcissist today? If yes, how did you respond?

_____

_____

_____

_____

_____

List a small goal that you will work towards accomplishing tomorrow:

_____

_____

_____

_____

_____

Date: ___/___/___

How are you feeling today? (Angry/*Depressed*/*Happy*/*Indifferent*/*Sick*)

_____

_____

_____

_____

_____

_____

Did you receive a Hoover from the Narcissist today? If yes, how did you respond?

_____

_____

_____

_____

_____

List a small goal that you will work towards accomplishing tomorrow:

_____

_____

_____

_____

_____

Date: ___/___/___

How are you feeling today? (Angry/*Depressed*/*Happy*/*Indifferent*/*Sick*)

_____

_____

_____

_____

_____

_____

_____

Did you receive a Hoover from the Narcissist today? If yes, how did you respond?

_____

_____

_____

_____

_____

List a small goal that you will work towards accomplishing tomorrow:

_____

_____

_____

_____

_____

_____

Date: ___/___/___

How are you feeling today? (Angry/*Depressed/Happy/Indifferent/Sick*)

_____

_____

_____

_____

_____

_____

_____

Did you receive a Hoover from the Narcissist today? If yes, how did you respond?

_____

_____

_____

_____

_____

_____

List a small goal that you will work towards accomplishing tomorrow:

_____

_____

_____

_____

_____

_____

Date: ___/___/___

How are you feeling today? (Angry/*Depressed/Happy/Indifferent/Sick*)

_____

_____

_____

_____

_____

_____

_____

Did you receive a Hoover from the Narcissist today? If yes, how did you respond?

_____

_____

_____

_____

_____

List a small goal that you will work towards accomplishing tomorrow:

_____

_____

_____

_____

_____

_____

Date: ___/___/___

How are you feeling today? (Angry/*Depressed/Happy/Indifferent/Sick*)

_____

_____

_____

_____

_____

_____

_____

Did you receive a Hoover from the Narcissist today? If yes, how did you respond?

_____

_____

_____

_____

_____

_____

List a small goal that you will work towards accomplishing tomorrow:

_____

_____

_____

_____

_____

_____

Date: ___/___/___

How are you feeling today? (Angry/*Depressed*/*Happy*/*Indifferent*/*Sick*)

_____

_____

_____

_____

_____

_____

Did you receive a Hoover from the Narcissist today? If yes, how did you respond?

_____

_____

_____

_____

_____

List a small goal that you will work towards accomplishing tomorrow:

_____

_____

_____

_____

_____

_____

Date: ___/___/___

How are you feeling today? (Angry/*Depressed*/*Happy*/*Indifferent*/*Sick*)

_____

_____

_____

_____

_____

_____

_____

Did you receive a Hoover from the Narcissist today? If yes, how did you respond?

_____

_____

_____

_____

_____

_____

List a small goal that you will work towards accomplishing tomorrow:

_____

_____

_____

_____

_____

Date: ___/___/___

How are you feeling today? (Angry/*Depressed*/*Happy*/*Indifferent*/*Sick*)

_____

_____

_____

_____

_____

_____

_____

Did you receive a Hoover from the Narcissist today? If yes, how did you respond?

_____

_____

_____

_____

_____

_____

List a small goal that you will work towards accomplishing tomorrow:

_____

_____

_____

_____

_____

_____

"When one door of happiness
closes, another opens, but often
we look so
long at the closed door that we
do not
see the one that has been opened
for us."
-Helen Keller

"Don't underestimate the value of
doing nothing, of just going along, listening to all the things you
can't hear, and not bothering."
-Winnie the Pooh

Date: ___/___/___

How are you feeling today? (Angry/*Depressed/Happy/Indifferent/Sick*)

_____

_____

_____

_____

_____

_____

_____

Did you receive a Hoover from the Narcissist today? If yes, how did you respond?

_____

_____

_____

_____

_____

List a small goal that you will work towards accomplishing tomorrow:

_____

_____

_____

_____

_____

Date: ___/___/___

How are you feeling today? (Angry/*Depressed/Happy/Indifferent/Sick*)

_____

_____

_____

_____

_____

_____

_____

Did you receive a Hoover from the Narcissist today? If yes, how did you respond?

_____

_____

_____

_____

_____

_____

List a small goal that you will work towards accomplishing tomorrow:

_____

_____

_____

_____

_____

_____

Date: ___/___/___

How are you feeling today? (Angry/*Depressed*/*Happy*/*Indifferent*/*Sick*)

_____

_____

_____

_____

_____

_____

Did you receive a Hoover from the Narcissist today? If yes, how did you respond?

_____

_____

_____

_____

_____

List a small goal that you will work towards accomplishing tomorrow:

_____

_____

_____

_____

_____

Date: ___/___/___

How are you feeling today? (Angry/*Depressed/Happy/Indifferent/Sick*)

_____

_____

_____

_____

_____

_____

Did you receive a Hoover from the Narcissist today? If yes, how did you respond?

_____

_____

_____

_____

_____

List a small goal that you will work towards accomplishing tomorrow:

_____

_____

_____

_____

_____

_____

Date: ___/___/___

How are you feeling today? (Angry/*Depressed*/*Happy*/*Indifferent*/*Sick*)

_____

_____

_____

_____

_____

_____

_____

Did you receive a Hoover from the Narcissist today? If yes, how did you respond?

_____

_____

_____

_____

_____

_____

List a small goal that you will work towards accomplishing tomorrow:

_____

_____

_____

_____

_____

_____

Date: ___/___/___

How are you feeling today? (Angry/*Depressed/Happy/Indifferent/Sick*)

_____

_____

_____

_____

_____

_____

_____

Did you receive a Hoover from the Narcissist today? If yes, how did you respond?

_____

_____

_____

_____

_____

List a small goal that you will work towards accomplishing tomorrow:

_____

_____

_____

_____

_____

Date: ___/___/___

How are you feeling today? (Angry/*Depressed*/*Happy*/*Indifferent*/*Sick*)

_____

_____

_____

_____

_____

_____

Did you receive a Hoover from the Narcissist today? If yes, how did you respond?

_____

_____

_____

_____

_____

List a small goal that you will work towards accomplishing tomorrow:

_____

_____

_____

_____

_____

Date: ___/___/___

How are you feeling today? (Angry/*Depressed/Happy/Indifferent/Sick*)

_____

_____

_____

_____

_____

_____

_____

Did you receive a Hoover from the Narcissist today? If yes, how did you respond?

_____

_____

_____

_____

_____

_____

List a small goal that you will work towards accomplishing tomorrow:

_____

_____

_____

_____

_____

_____

Date: ___/___/___

How are you feeling today? (Angry/*Depressed*/*Happy*/*Indifferent*/*Sick*)

_____

_____

_____

_____

_____

_____

Did you receive a Hoover from the Narcissist today? If yes, how did you respond?

_____

_____

_____

_____

_____

List a small goal that you will work towards accomplishing tomorrow:

_____

_____

_____

_____

_____

Date: ___/___/___

How are you feeling today? (Angry/*Depressed/Happy/Indifferent/Sick*)

_____

_____

_____

_____

_____

_____

_____

Did you receive a Hoover from the Narcissist today? If yes, how did you respond?

_____

_____

_____

_____

_____

List a small goal that you will work towards accomplishing tomorrow:

_____

_____

_____

_____

_____

_____

Date: ___/___/___

How are you feeling today? (Angry/*Depressed/Happy/Indifferent/Sick*)

_____

_____

_____

_____

_____

_____

Did you receive a Hoover from the Narcissist today? If yes, how did you respond?

_____

_____

_____

_____

_____

List a small goal that you will work towards accomplishing tomorrow:

_____

_____

_____

_____

_____

Date: ___/___/___

How are you feeling today? (Angry/*Depressed/Happy/Indifferent/Sick*)

_____

_____

_____

_____

_____

_____

_____

Did you receive a Hoover from the Narcissist today? If yes, how did you respond?

_____

_____

_____

_____

_____

_____

List a small goal that you will work towards accomplishing tomorrow:

_____

_____

_____

_____

_____

_____

Date: ___/___/___

How are you feeling today? (Angry/*Depressed*/*Happy*/*Indifferent*/*Sick*)

_____

_____

_____

_____

_____

_____

_____

Did you receive a Hoover from the Narcissist today? If yes, how did you respond?

_____

_____

_____

_____

_____

_____

List a small goal that you will work towards accomplishing tomorrow:

_____

_____

_____

_____

_____

_____

Date: ___/___/___

How are you feeling today? (Angry/*Depressed/Happy/Indifferent/Sick*)

_____

_____

_____

_____

_____

_____

_____

Did you receive a Hoover from the Narcissist today? If yes, how did you respond?

_____

_____

_____

_____

_____

_____

List a small goal that you will work towards accomplishing tomorrow:

_____

_____

_____

_____

_____

_____

Date: ___/___/___

How are you feeling today? (Angry/*Depressed*/*Happy*/*Indifferent*/*Sick*)

_____

_____

_____

_____

_____

_____

_____

Did you receive a Hoover from the Narcissist today? If yes, how did you respond?

_____

_____

_____

_____

_____

_____

List a small goal that you will work towards accomplishing tomorrow:

_____

_____

_____

_____

_____

_____

Date: ___/___/___

How are you feeling today? (Angry/*Depressed*/*Happy*/*Indifferent*/*Sick*)

_____

_____

_____

_____

_____

_____

Did you receive a Hoover from the Narcissist today? If yes, how did you respond?

_____

_____

_____

_____

_____

List a small goal that you will work towards accomplishing tomorrow:

_____

_____

_____

_____

_____

_____

Date: ___/___/___

How are you feeling today? (Angry/*Depressed*/*Happy*/*Indifferent*/*Sick*)

_____

_____

_____

_____

_____

_____

Did you receive a Hoover from the Narcissist today? If yes, how did you respond?

_____

_____

_____

_____

_____

List a small goal that you will work towards accomplishing tomorrow:

_____

_____

_____

_____

_____

Date: ___/___/___

How are you feeling today? (Angry/*Depressed/Happy/Indifferent/Sick*)

_____

_____

_____

_____

_____

_____

_____

Did you receive a Hoover from the Narcissist today? If yes, how did you respond?

_____

_____

_____

_____

_____

List a small goal that you will work towards accomplishing tomorrow:

_____

_____

_____

_____

_____

_____

Date: ___/___/___

How are you feeling today? (Angry/*Depressed*/*Happy*/*Indifferent*/*Sick*)

_____

_____

_____

_____

_____

_____

_____

Did you receive a Hoover from the Narcissist today? If yes, how did you respond?

_____

_____

_____

_____

_____

_____

List a small goal that you will work towards accomplishing tomorrow:

_____

_____

_____

_____

_____

_____

Date: ___/___/___

How are you feeling today? (Angry/*Depressed/Happy/Indifferent/Sick*)

_____

_____

_____

_____

_____

_____

_____

_____

Did you receive a Hoover from the Narcissist today? If yes, how did you respond?

_____

_____

_____

_____

_____

_____

List a small goal that you will work towards accomplishing tomorrow:

_____

_____

_____

_____

_____

_____

Date: ___/___/___

How are you feeling today? (Angry/*Depressed*/*Happy*/*Indifferent*/*Sick*)

_____

_____

_____

_____

_____

_____

_____

Did you receive a Hoover from the Narcissist today? If yes, how did you respond?

_____

_____

_____

_____

_____

_____

List a small goal that you will work towards accomplishing tomorrow:

_____

_____

_____

_____

_____

_____

Date: ___/___/___

How are you feeling today? (Angry/*Depressed*/*Happy*/*Indifferent*/*Sick*)

_____

_____

_____

_____

_____

_____

_____

Did you receive a Hoover from the Narcissist today? If yes, how did you respond?

_____

_____

_____

_____

_____

_____

List a small goal that you will work towards accomplishing tomorrow:

_____

_____

_____

_____

_____

_____

Date: ___/___/___

How are you feeling today? (Angry/*Depressed/Happy/Indifferent/Sick*)

_____

_____

_____

_____

_____

_____

_____

Did you receive a Hoover from the Narcissist today? If yes, how did you respond?

_____

_____

_____

_____

_____

_____

List a small goal that you will work towards accomplishing tomorrow:

_____

_____

_____

_____

_____

_____

Date: ___/___/___

How are you feeling today? (Angry/*Depressed/Happy/Indifferent/Sick*)

_____

_____

_____

_____

_____

_____

_____

Did you receive a Hoover from the Narcissist today? If yes, how did you respond?

_____

_____

_____

_____

_____

List a small goal that you will work towards accomplishing tomorrow:

_____

_____

_____

_____

_____

Date: ___/___/___

How are you feeling today? (Angry/*Depressed*/*Happy*/*Indifferent*/*Sick*)

_____

_____

_____

_____

_____

_____

Did you receive a Hoover from the Narcissist today? If yes, how did you respond?

_____

_____

_____

_____

_____

List a small goal that you will work towards accomplishing tomorrow:

_____

_____

_____

_____

_____

Date: ___/___/___

How are you feeling today? (Angry/*Depressed*/*Happy*/*Indifferent*/*Sick*)

_____

_____

_____

_____

_____

_____

_____

Did you receive a Hoover from the Narcissist today? If yes, how did you respond?

_____

_____

_____

_____

_____

_____

List a small goal that you will work towards accomplishing tomorrow:

_____

_____

_____

_____

_____

_____

Date: ___/___/___

How are you feeling today? (Angry/*Depressed*/*Happy*/*Indifferent*/*Sick*)

_____

_____

_____

_____

_____

_____

_____

Did you receive a Hoover from the Narcissist today? If yes, how did you respond?

_____

_____

_____

_____

_____

_____

List a small goal that you will work towards accomplishing tomorrow:

_____

_____

_____

_____

_____

_____

Date: ___/___/___

How are you feeling today? (Angry/*Depressed/Happy/Indifferent/Sick*)

_____

_____

_____

_____

_____

_____

Did you receive a Hoover from the Narcissist today? If yes, how did you respond?

_____

_____

_____

_____

_____

List a small goal that you will work towards accomplishing tomorrow:

_____

_____

_____

_____

_____

Date: ___/___/___

How are you feeling today? (Angry/*Depressed/Happy/Indifferent/Sick*)

_____

_____

_____

_____

_____

_____

_____

Did you receive a Hoover from the Narcissist today? If yes, how did you respond?

_____

_____

_____

_____

_____

_____

List a small goal that you will work towards accomplishing tomorrow:

_____

_____

_____

_____

_____

_____

Date: ___/___/___

How are you feeling today? (Angry/*Depressed/Happy/Indifferent/Sick*)

_____

_____

_____

_____

_____

_____

_____

Did you receive a Hoover from the Narcissist today? If yes, how did you respond?

_____

_____

_____

_____

_____

List a small goal that you will work towards accomplishing tomorrow:

_____

_____

_____

_____

_____

_____

Date: ___/___/___

How are you feeling today? (Angry/*Depressed/Happy/Indifferent/Sick*)

_____

_____

_____

_____

_____

_____

Did you receive a Hoover from the Narcissist today? If yes, how did you respond?

_____

_____

_____

_____

_____

List a small goal that you will work towards accomplishing tomorrow:

_____

_____

_____

_____

_____

Date: ___/___/___

How are you feeling today? (Angry/*Depressed/Happy/Indifferent/Sick*)

_____

_____

_____

_____

_____

_____

_____

Did you receive a Hoover from the Narcissist today? If yes, how did you respond?

_____

_____

_____

_____

_____

_____

List a small goal that you will work towards accomplishing tomorrow:

_____

_____

_____

_____

_____

_____

Date: ___/___/___

How are you feeling today? (Angry/*Depressed/Happy/Indifferent/Sick*)

_____

_____

_____

_____

_____

_____

Did you receive a Hoover from the Narcissist today? If yes, how did you respond?

_____

_____

_____

_____

_____

List a small goal that you will work towards accomplishing tomorrow:

_____

_____

_____

_____

_____

Date: ___/___/___

How are you feeling today? (Angry/*Depressed*/*Happy*/*Indifferent*/*Sick*)

_____

_____

_____

_____

_____

_____

_____

Did you receive a Hoover from the Narcissist today? If yes, how did you respond?

_____

_____

_____

_____

_____

_____

List a small goal that you will work towards accomplishing tomorrow:

_____

_____

_____

_____

_____

_____

Date: ___/___/___

How are you feeling today? (Angry/*Depressed*/*Happy*/*Indifferent*/*Sick*)

_____

_____

_____

_____

_____

_____

_____

Did you receive a Hoover from the Narcissist today? If yes, how did you respond?

_____

_____

_____

_____

_____

_____

List a small goal that you will work towards accomplishing tomorrow:

_____

_____

_____

_____

_____

_____

Date: ___/___/___

How are you feeling today? (Angry/*Depressed/Happy/Indifferent/Sick*)

_____

_____

_____

_____

_____

_____

_____

Did you receive a Hoover from the Narcissist today? If yes, how did you respond?

_____

_____

_____

_____

_____

_____

List a small goal that you will work towards accomplishing tomorrow:

_____

_____

_____

_____

_____

"The more you know who you are, and what you want, the less you let things upset you."
-Stephanie Perkins

"Until you value yourself, you won't value your time. Until you value your time, you will not do anything with it."
-M. Scott Peck

Date: ___/___/___

How are you feeling today? (Angry/*Depressed*/*Happy*/*Indifferent*/*Sick*)

_____

_____

_____

_____

_____

_____

Did you receive a Hoover from the Narcissist today? If yes, how did you respond?

_____

_____

_____

_____

_____

List a small goal that you will work towards accomplishing tomorrow:

_____

_____

_____

_____

_____

_____

Date: ___/___/___

How are you feeling today? (Angry/*Depressed*/*Happy*/*Indifferent*/*Sick*)

_____

_____

_____

_____

_____

_____

_____

Did you receive a Hoover from the Narcissist today? If yes, how did you respond?

_____

_____

_____

_____

_____

List a small goal that you will work towards accomplishing tomorrow:

_____

_____

_____

_____

_____

_____

Date: ___/___/___

How are you feeling today? (Angry/*Depressed*/*Happy*/*Indifferent*/*Sick*)

_____

_____

_____

_____

_____

_____

_____

Did you receive a Hoover from the Narcissist today? If yes, how did you respond?

_____

_____

_____

_____

_____

_____

List a small goal that you will work towards accomplishing tomorrow:

_____

_____

_____

_____

_____

_____

Date: ___/___/___

How are you feeling today? (Angry/*Depressed/Happy/Indifferent/Sick*)

_____

_____

_____

_____

_____

_____

_____

Did you receive a Hoover from the Narcissist today? If yes, how did you respond?

_____

_____

_____

_____

_____

_____

List a small goal that you will work towards accomplishing tomorrow:

_____

_____

_____

_____

_____

_____

_____

Date: ___/___/___

How are you feeling today? (Angry/*Depressed/Happy/Indifferent/Sick*)

_____

_____

_____

_____

_____

_____

_____

Did you receive a Hoover from the Narcissist today? If yes, how did you respond?

_____

_____

_____

_____

_____

_____

List a small goal that you will work towards accomplishing tomorrow:

_____

_____

_____

_____

_____

_____

Date: ___/___/___

How are you feeling today? (Angry/*Depressed/Happy/Indifferent/Sick*)

_____

_____

_____

_____

_____

_____

_____

Did you receive a Hoover from the Narcissist today? If yes, how did you respond?

_____

_____

_____

_____

_____

_____

List a small goal that you will work towards accomplishing tomorrow:

_____

_____

_____

_____

_____

Date: ___/___/___

How are you feeling today? (Angry/*Depressed*/*Happy*/*Indifferent*/*Sick*)

_____

_____

_____

_____

_____

_____

Did you receive a Hoover from the Narcissist today? If yes, how did you respond?

_____

_____

_____

_____

_____

List a small goal that you will work towards accomplishing tomorrow:

_____

_____

_____

_____

_____

Date: ___/___/___

How are you feeling today? (Angry/*Depressed/Happy/Indifferent/Sick*)

_____

_____

_____

_____

_____

_____

_____

_____

Did you receive a Hoover from the Narcissist today? If yes, how did you respond?

_____

_____

_____

_____

_____

_____

List a small goal that you will work towards accomplishing tomorrow:

_____

_____

_____

_____

_____

_____

Date: ___/___/___

How are you feeling today? (Angry/*Depressed/Happy/Indifferent/Sick*)

_____

_____

_____

_____

_____

_____

_____

Did you receive a Hoover from the Narcissist today? If yes, how did you respond?

_____

_____

_____

_____

_____

_____

List a small goal that you will work towards accomplishing tomorrow:

_____

_____

_____

_____

_____

Date: ___/___/___

How are you feeling today? (Angry/*Depressed*/*Happy*/*Indifferent*/*Sick*)

_____

_____

_____

_____

_____

_____

Did you receive a Hoover from the Narcissist today? If yes, how did you respond?

_____

_____

_____

_____

_____

List a small goal that you will work towards accomplishing tomorrow:

_____

_____

_____

_____

_____

Date: ___/___/___

How are you feeling today? (Angry/*Depressed/Happy/Indifferent/Sick*)

_____

_____

_____

_____

_____

_____

_____

Did you receive a Hoover from the Narcissist today? If yes, how did you respond?

_____

_____

_____

_____

_____

_____

List a small goal that you will work towards accomplishing tomorrow:

_____

_____

_____

_____

_____

_____

Date: ___/___/___

How are you feeling today? (Angry/*Depressed/Happy/Indifferent/Sick*)

_____

_____

_____

_____

_____

_____

_____

Did you receive a Hoover from the Narcissist today? If yes, how did you respond?

_____

_____

_____

_____

_____

List a small goal that you will work towards accomplishing tomorrow:

_____

_____

_____

_____

_____

_____

Date: ___/___/___

How are you feeling today? (Angry/*Depressed*/*Happy*/*Indifferent*/*Sick*)

_____

_____

_____

_____

_____

_____

Did you receive a Hoover from the Narcissist today? If yes, how did you respond?

_____

_____

_____

_____

_____

List a small goal that you will work towards accomplishing tomorrow:

_____

_____

_____

_____

_____

Date: ___/___/___

How are you feeling today? (Angry/*Depressed*/*Happy*/*Indifferent*/*Sick*)

_____

_____

_____

_____

_____

_____

_____

Did you receive a Hoover from the Narcissist today? If yes, how did you respond?

_____

_____

_____

_____

_____

_____

List a small goal that you will work towards accomplishing tomorrow:

_____

_____

_____

_____

_____

_____

Date: ___/___/___

How are you feeling today? (Angry/*Depressed/Happy/Indifferent/Sick*)

_____
_____
_____
_____
_____
_____
_____

Did you receive a Hoover from the Narcissist today? If yes, how did you respond?

_____
_____
_____
_____
_____
_____

List a small goal that you will work towards accomplishing tomorrow:

_____
_____
_____
_____
_____
_____

Date: ___/___/___

How are you feeling today? (Angry/*Depressed/Happy/Indifferent/Sick*)

_____

_____

_____

_____

_____

_____

_____

Did you receive a Hoover from the Narcissist today? If yes, how did you respond?

_____

_____

_____

_____

_____

List a small goal that you will work towards accomplishing tomorrow:

_____

_____

_____

_____

_____

_____

"The way to love anything is to realize that it may be lost."
-Gilbert K. Chesterton

"If you aren't good at loving yourself, you will have a difficult time loving anyone, since you'll resent the time and energy you give another person that you aren't even giving to yourself."
-Barbara De Angelis

Date: ___/___/___

How are you feeling today? (Angry/*Depressed*/*Happy*/*Indifferent*/*Sick*)

_____

_____

_____

_____

_____

_____

Did you receive a Hoover from the Narcissist today? If yes, how did you respond?

_____

_____

_____

_____

_____

List a small goal that you will work towards accomplishing tomorrow:

_____

_____

_____

_____

_____

_____

Date: ___/___/___

How are you feeling today? (Angry/*Depressed*/*Happy*/*Indifferent*/*Sick*)

_____

_____

_____

_____

_____

_____

_____

Did you receive a Hoover from the Narcissist today? If yes, how did you respond?

_____

_____

_____

_____

_____

_____

List a small goal that you will work towards accomplishing tomorrow:

_____

_____

_____

_____

_____

_____

Date: ___/___/___

How are you feeling today? (Angry/*Depressed*/*Happy*/*Indifferent*/*Sick*)

_____

_____

_____

_____

_____

_____

_____

Did you receive a Hoover from the Narcissist today? If yes, how did you respond?

_____

_____

_____

_____

_____

_____

List a small goal that you will work towards accomplishing tomorrow:

_____

_____

_____

_____

_____

_____

Date: ___/___/___

How are you feeling today? (Angry/*Depressed/Happy/Indifferent/Sick*)

_____

_____

_____

_____

_____

_____

Did you receive a Hoover from the Narcissist today? If yes, how did you respond?

_____

_____

_____

_____

_____

List a small goal that you will work towards accomplishing tomorrow:

_____

_____

_____

_____

_____

Date: ___/___/___

How are you feeling today? (Angry/*Depressed/Happy/Indifferent/Sick*)

_____

_____

_____

_____

_____

_____

Did you receive a Hoover from the Narcissist today? If yes, how did you respond?

_____

_____

_____

_____

_____

_____

List a small goal that you will work towards accomplishing tomorrow:

_____

_____

_____

_____

_____

_____

Date: ___/___/___

How are you feeling today? (Angry/*Depressed/Happy/Indifferent/Sick*)

_____

_____

_____

_____

_____

_____

_____

Did you receive a Hoover from the Narcissist today? If yes, how did you respond?

_____

_____

_____

_____

_____

List a small goal that you will work towards accomplishing tomorrow:

_____

_____

_____

_____

_____

_____

Date: ___/___/___

How are you feeling today? (Angry/*Depressed*/*Happy*/*Indifferent*/*Sick*)

_____

_____

_____

_____

_____

_____

_____

Did you receive a Hoover from the Narcissist today? If yes, how did you respond?

_____

_____

_____

_____

_____

_____

List a small goal that you will work towards accomplishing tomorrow:

_____

_____

_____

_____

_____

_____

Date: ___/___/___

How are you feeling today? (Angry/*Depressed*/*Happy*/*Indifferent*/*Sick*)

_____

_____

_____

_____

_____

_____

_____

Did you receive a Hoover from the Narcissist today? If yes, how did you respond?

_____

_____

_____

_____

_____

_____

List a small goal that you will work towards accomplishing tomorrow:

_____

_____

_____

_____

_____

_____

Date: ___/___/___

How are you feeling today? (Angry/*Depressed/Happy/Indifferent/Sick*)

_____

_____

_____

_____

_____

_____

Did you receive a Hoover from the Narcissist today? If yes, how did you respond?

_____

_____

_____

_____

_____

List a small goal that you will work towards accomplishing tomorrow:

_____

_____

_____

_____

_____

_____

Date: ___/___/___

How are you feeling today? (Angry/*Depressed/Happy/Indifferent/Sick*)

_____
_____
_____
_____
_____
_____
_____

Did you receive a Hoover from the Narcissist today? If yes, how did you respond?

_____
_____
_____
_____
_____

List a small goal that you will work towards accomplishing tomorrow:

_____
_____
_____
_____
_____

Date: ___/___/___

How are you feeling today? (Angry/*Depressed*/*Happy*/*Indifferent*/*Sick*)

_____

_____

_____

_____

_____

_____

_____

Did you receive a Hoover from the Narcissist today? If yes, how did you respond?

_____

_____

_____

_____

_____

_____

List a small goal that you will work towards accomplishing tomorrow:

_____

_____

_____

_____

_____

_____

Date: ___/___/___

How are you feeling today? (Angry/*Depressed*/*Happy*/*Indifferent*/*Sick*)

_____

_____

_____

_____

_____

_____

_____

Did you receive a Hoover from the Narcissist today? If yes, how did you respond?

_____

_____

_____

_____

_____

List a small goal that you will work towards accomplishing tomorrow:

_____

_____

_____

_____

_____

Date: ___/___/___

How are you feeling today? (Angry/*Depressed/Happy/Indifferent/Sick*)

_____

_____

_____

_____

_____

_____

Did you receive a Hoover from the Narcissist today? If yes, how did you respond?

_____

_____

_____

_____

_____

_____

List a small goal that you will work towards accomplishing tomorrow:

_____

_____

_____

_____

_____

_____

Date: ___/___/___

How are you feeling today? (Angry/*Depressed/Happy/Indifferent/Sick*)

_____

_____

_____

_____

_____

_____

_____

Did you receive a Hoover from the Narcissist today? If yes, how did you respond?

_____

_____

_____

_____

_____

List a small goal that you will work towards accomplishing tomorrow:

_____

_____

_____

_____

_____

_____

Date: ___/___/___

How are you feeling today? (Angry/*Depressed/Happy/Indifferent/Sick*)

_____

_____

_____

_____

_____

_____

Did you receive a Hoover from the Narcissist today? If yes, how did you respond?

_____

_____

_____

_____

_____

List a small goal that you will work towards accomplishing tomorrow:

_____

_____

_____

_____

_____

_____

Date: ___/___/___

How are you feeling today? (Angry/*Depressed/Happy/Indifferent/Sick*)

_____

_____

_____

_____

_____

_____

_____

Did you receive a Hoover from the Narcissist today? If yes, how did you respond?

_____

_____

_____

_____

_____

List a small goal that you will work towards accomplishing tomorrow:

_____

_____

_____

_____

_____

_____

Date: ___/___/___

How are you feeling today? (Angry/*Depressed*/*Happy*/*Indifferent*/*Sick*)

_____

_____

_____

_____

_____

_____

_____

Did you receive a Hoover from the Narcissist today? If yes, how did you respond?

_____

_____

_____

_____

_____

List a small goal that you will work towards accomplishing tomorrow:

_____

_____

_____

_____

_____

Date: ___/___/___

How are you feeling today? (Angry/*Depressed*/*Happy*/*Indifferent*/*Sick*)

_____

_____

_____

_____

_____

_____

_____

Did you receive a Hoover from the Narcissist today? If yes, how did you respond?

_____

_____

_____

_____

_____

_____

List a small goal that you will work towards accomplishing tomorrow:

_____

_____

_____

_____

_____

_____

Date: ___/___/___

How are you feeling today? (Angry/*Depressed*/*Happy*/*Indifferent*/*Sick*)

_____

_____

_____

_____

_____

_____

_____

Did you receive a Hoover from the Narcissist today? If yes, how did you respond?

_____

_____

_____

_____

_____

List a small goal that you will work towards accomplishing tomorrow:

_____

_____

_____

_____

_____

Date: ___/___/___

How are you feeling today? (Angry/*Depressed/Happy/Indifferent/Sick*)

_____

_____

_____

_____

_____

_____

_____

_____

Did you receive a Hoover from the Narcissist today? If yes, how did you respond?

_____

_____

_____

_____

_____

_____

_____

List a small goal that you will work towards accomplishing tomorrow:

_____

_____

_____

_____

_____

_____

_____

Date: ___/___/___

How are you feeling today? (Angry/*Depressed/Happy/Indifferent/Sick*)

_____

_____

_____

_____

_____

_____

_____

Did you receive a Hoover from the Narcissist today? If yes, how did you respond?

_____

_____

_____

_____

_____

_____

List a small goal that you will work towards accomplishing tomorrow:

_____

_____

_____

_____

_____

_____

Date: ___/___/___

How are you feeling today? (Angry/*Depressed/Happy/Indifferent/Sick*)

_____

_____

_____

_____

_____

_____

Did you receive a Hoover from the Narcissist today? If yes, how did you respond?

_____

_____

_____

_____

_____

List a small goal that you will work towards accomplishing tomorrow:

_____

_____

_____

_____

_____

Date: ___/___/___

How are you feeling today? (Angry/*Depressed*/*Happy*/*Indifferent*/*Sick*)

_____

_____

_____

_____

_____

_____

_____

Did you receive a Hoover from the Narcissist today? If yes, how did you respond?

_____

_____

_____

_____

_____

_____

List a small goal that you will work towards accomplishing tomorrow:

_____

_____

_____

_____

_____

_____

Date: ___/___/___

How are you feeling today? (Angry/*Depressed/Happy/Indifferent/Sick*)

_____

_____

_____

_____

_____

_____

Did you receive a Hoover from the Narcissist today? If yes, how did you respond?

_____

_____

_____

_____

_____

List a small goal that you will work towards accomplishing tomorrow:

_____

_____

_____

_____

_____

Date: ___/___/___

How are you feeling today? (Angry/*Depressed/Happy/Indifferent/Sick*)

_____

_____

_____

_____

_____

_____

Did you receive a Hoover from the Narcissist today? If yes, how did you respond?

_____

_____

_____

_____

_____

List a small goal that you will work towards accomplishing tomorrow:

_____

_____

_____

_____

_____

Date: ___/___/___

How are you feeling today? (Angry/*Depressed/Happy/Indifferent/Sick*)

_____

_____

_____

_____

_____

_____

Did you receive a Hoover from the Narcissist today? If yes, how did you respond?

_____

_____

_____

_____

_____

List a small goal that you will work towards accomplishing tomorrow:

_____

_____

_____

_____

_____

Date: ___/___/___

How are you feeling today? (Angry/*Depressed/Happy/Indifferent/Sick*)

_____

_____

_____

_____

_____

_____

Did you receive a Hoover from the Narcissist today? If yes, how did you respond?

_____

_____

_____

_____

_____

List a small goal that you will work towards accomplishing tomorrow:

_____

_____

_____

_____

_____

Date: ___/___/___

How are you feeling today? (Angry/*Depressed/Happy/Indifferent/Sick*)

_____

_____

_____

_____

_____

_____

_____

Did you receive a Hoover from the Narcissist today? If yes, how did you respond?

_____

_____

_____

_____

_____

_____

List a small goal that you will work towards accomplishing tomorrow:

_____

_____

_____

_____

_____

_____

Date: ___/___/___

How are you feeling today? (Angry/*Depressed/Happy/Indifferent/Sick*)

_____

_____

_____

_____

_____

_____

_____

Did you receive a Hoover from the Narcissist today? If yes, how did you respond?

_____

_____

_____

_____

_____

_____

List a small goal that you will work towards accomplishing tomorrow:

_____

_____

_____

_____

_____

_____

Date: ___/___/___

How are you feeling today? (Angry/*Depressed/Happy/Indifferent/Sick*)

_____
_____
_____
_____
_____
_____
_____

Did you receive a Hoover from the Narcissist today? If yes, how did you respond?

_____
_____
_____
_____
_____
_____

List a small goal that you will work towards accomplishing tomorrow:

_____
_____
_____
_____
_____
_____
_____

"Now may the Lord of peace himself give you peace at all times and in every way. The Lord be with all of you."

-2 Thessalonians 3:16

"For with God nothing shall
be impossible."
-Luke 1:37

Date: ___/___/___

How are you feeling today? (Angry/*Depressed/Happy/Indifferent/Sick*)

_____

_____

_____

_____

_____

_____

_____

Did you receive a Hoover from the Narcissist today? If yes, how did you respond?

_____

_____

_____

_____

_____

_____

List a small goal that you will work towards accomplishing tomorrow:

_____

_____

_____

_____

_____

_____

Date: ___/___/___

How are you feeling today? (Angry/*Depressed/Happy/Indifferent/Sick*)

_____

_____

_____

_____

_____

_____

_____

Did you receive a Hoover from the Narcissist today? If yes, how did you respond?

_____

_____

_____

_____

_____

List a small goal that you will work towards accomplishing tomorrow:

_____

_____

_____

_____

_____

_____

Date: ___/___/___

How are you feeling today? (Angry/*Depressed/Happy/Indifferent/Sick*)

_____

_____

_____

_____

_____

_____

_____

Did you receive a Hoover from the Narcissist today? If yes, how did you respond?

_____

_____

_____

_____

_____

_____

List a small goal that you will work towards accomplishing tomorrow:

_____

_____

_____

_____

_____

_____

Date: ___/___/___

How are you feeling today? (Angry/*Depressed/Happy/Indifferent/Sick*)

_____

_____

_____

_____

_____

_____

_____

Did you receive a Hoover from the Narcissist today? If yes, how did you respond?

_____

_____

_____

_____

_____

_____

List a small goal that you will work towards accomplishing tomorrow:

_____

_____

_____

_____

_____

_____

_____

Date: ___/___/___

How are you feeling today? (Angry/*Depressed*/*Happy*/*Indifferent*/*Sick*)

_____

_____

_____

_____

_____

_____

Did you receive a Hoover from the Narcissist today? If yes, how did you respond?

_____

_____

_____

_____

_____

List a small goal that you will work towards accomplishing tomorrow:

_____

_____

_____

_____

_____

Date: ___/___/___

How are you feeling today? (Angry/*Depressed*/*Happy*/*Indifferent*/*Sick*)

_____

_____

_____

_____

_____

_____

_____

Did you receive a Hoover from the Narcissist today? If yes, how did you respond?

_____

_____

_____

_____

_____

_____

List a small goal that you will work towards accomplishing tomorrow:

_____

_____

_____

_____

_____

_____

Date: ___/___/___

How are you feeling today? (Angry/*Depressed*/*Happy*/*Indifferent*/*Sick*)

_____

_____

_____

_____

_____

_____

_____

Did you receive a Hoover from the Narcissist today? If yes, how did you respond?

_____

_____

_____

_____

_____

_____

List a small goal that you will work towards accomplishing tomorrow:

_____

_____

_____

_____

_____

_____

Date: ___/___/___

How are you feeling today? (Angry/*Depressed/Happy/Indifferent/Sick*)

_____

_____

_____

_____

_____

_____

_____

Did you receive a Hoover from the Narcissist today? If yes, how did you respond?

_____

_____

_____

_____

_____

_____

List a small goal that you will work towards accomplishing tomorrow:

_____

_____

_____

_____

_____

_____

Date: ___/___/___

How are you feeling today? (Angry/*Depressed/Happy/Indifferent/Sick*)

_____

_____

_____

_____

_____

_____

_____

Did you receive a Hoover from the Narcissist today? If yes, how did you respond?

_____

_____

_____

_____

_____

_____

List a small goal that you will work towards accomplishing tomorrow:

_____

_____

_____

_____

_____

_____

Date: ___/___/___

How are you feeling today? (Angry/*Depressed/Happy/Indifferent/Sick*)

_____

_____

_____

_____

_____

_____

_____

Did you receive a Hoover from the Narcissist today? If yes, how did you respond?

_____

_____

_____

_____

_____

_____

List a small goal that you will work towards accomplishing tomorrow:

_____

_____

_____

_____

_____

_____

Date: ___/___/___

How are you feeling today? (Angry/*Depressed*/*Happy*/*Indifferent*/*Sick*)

_____

_____

_____

_____

_____

_____

Did you receive a Hoover from the Narcissist today? If yes, how did you respond?

_____

_____

_____

_____

_____

List a small goal that you will work towards accomplishing tomorrow:

_____

_____

_____

_____

_____

Date: ___/___/___

How are you feeling today? (Angry/*Depressed/Happy/Indifferent/Sick*)

_____

_____

_____

_____

_____

_____

Did you receive a Hoover from the Narcissist today? If yes, how did you respond?

_____

_____

_____

_____

_____

List a small goal that you will work towards accomplishing tomorrow:

_____

_____

_____

_____

_____

_____

Date: ___/___/___

How are you feeling today? (Angry/*Depressed*/*Happy*/*Indifferent*/*Sick*)

_____

_____

_____

_____

_____

_____

_____

Did you receive a Hoover from the Narcissist today? If yes, how did you respond?

_____

_____

_____

_____

_____

_____

List a small goal that you will work towards accomplishing tomorrow:

_____

_____

_____

_____

_____

_____

Date: ___/___/___

How are you feeling today? (Angry/*Depressed*/*Happy*/*Indifferent*/*Sick*)

_____

_____

_____

_____

_____

_____

_____

Did you receive a Hoover from the Narcissist today? If yes, how did you respond?

_____

_____

_____

_____

_____

_____

List a small goal that you will work towards accomplishing tomorrow:

_____

_____

_____

_____

_____

_____

Date: ___/___/___

How are you feeling today? (Angry/*Depressed/Happy/Indifferent/Sick*)

_____

_____

_____

_____

_____

_____

_____

Did you receive a Hoover from the Narcissist today? If yes, how did you respond?

_____

_____

_____

_____

_____

_____

List a small goal that you will work towards accomplishing tomorrow:

_____

_____

_____

_____

_____

_____

Date: ___/___/___

How are you feeling today? (Angry/*Depressed/Happy/Indifferent/Sick*)

_____

_____

_____

_____

_____

_____

Did you receive a Hoover from the Narcissist today? If yes, how did you respond?

_____

_____

_____

_____

_____

List a small goal that you will work towards accomplishing tomorrow:

_____

_____

_____

_____

_____

_____

Date: ___/___/___

How are you feeling today? (Angry/*Depressed*/*Happy*/*Indifferent*/*Sick*)

_____

_____

_____

_____

_____

_____

_____

Did you receive a Hoover from the Narcissist today? If yes, how did you respond?

_____

_____

_____

_____

_____

_____

List a small goal that you will work towards accomplishing tomorrow:

_____

_____

_____

_____

_____

_____

Date: ___/___/___

How are you feeling today? (Angry/*Depressed/Happy/Indifferent/Sick*)

_____

_____

_____

_____

_____

_____

_____

Did you receive a Hoover from the Narcissist today? If yes, how did you respond?

_____

_____

_____

_____

_____

_____

List a small goal that you will work towards accomplishing tomorrow:

_____

_____

_____

_____

_____

_____

Date: ___/___/___

How are you feeling today? (Angry/*Depressed/Happy/Indifferent/Sick*)

_____

_____

_____

_____

_____

_____

Did you receive a Hoover from the Narcissist today? If yes, how did you respond?

_____

_____

_____

_____

_____

List a small goal that you will work towards accomplishing tomorrow:

_____

_____

_____

_____

_____

_____

Date: ___/___/___

How are you feeling today? (Angry/*Depressed*/*Happy*/*Indifferent*/*Sick*)

_____

_____

_____

_____

_____

_____

Did you receive a Hoover from the Narcissist today? If yes, how did you respond?

_____

_____

_____

_____

_____

List a small goal that you will work towards accomplishing tomorrow:

_____

_____

_____

_____

_____

Date: ___/___/___

How are you feeling today? (Angry/*Depressed*/*Happy*/*Indifferent*/*Sick*)

_____

_____

_____

_____

_____

_____

_____

Did you receive a Hoover from the Narcissist today? If yes, how did you respond?

_____

_____

_____

_____

_____

_____

List a small goal that you will work towards accomplishing tomorrow:

_____

_____

_____

_____

_____

Date: ___/___/___

How are you feeling today? (Angry/*Depressed/Happy/Indifferent/Sick*)

_____

_____

_____

_____

_____

_____

_____

Did you receive a Hoover from the Narcissist today? If yes, how did you respond?

_____

_____

_____

_____

_____

_____

List a small goal that you will work towards accomplishing tomorrow:

_____

_____

_____

_____

_____

_____

Date: ___/___/___

How are you feeling today? (Angry/*Depressed*/*Happy*/*Indifferent*/*Sick*)

_____

_____

_____

_____

_____

_____

Did you receive a Hoover from the Narcissist today? If yes, how did you respond?

_____

_____

_____

_____

_____

List a small goal that you will work towards accomplishing tomorrow:

_____

_____

_____

_____

_____

Date: ___/___/___

How are you feeling today? (Angry/*Depressed/Happy/Indifferent/Sick*)

_____

_____

_____

_____

_____

_____

Did you receive a Hoover from the Narcissist today? If yes, how did you respond?

_____

_____

_____

_____

_____

List a small goal that you will work towards accomplishing tomorrow:

_____

_____

_____

_____

_____

Date: ___/___/___

How are you feeling today? (Angry/*Depressed*/*Happy*/*Indifferent*/*Sick*)

_____

_____

_____

_____

_____

_____

Did you receive a Hoover from the Narcissist today? If yes, how did you respond?

_____

_____

_____

_____

_____

List a small goal that you will work towards accomplishing tomorrow:

_____

_____

_____

_____

_____

Date: ___/___/___

How are you feeling today? (Angry/*Depressed/Happy/Indifferent/Sick*)

_____

_____

_____

_____

_____

_____

Did you receive a Hoover from the Narcissist today? If yes, how did you respond?

_____

_____

_____

_____

_____

List a small goal that you will work towards accomplishing tomorrow:

_____

_____

_____

_____

_____

Date: ___/___/___

How are you feeling today? (Angry/*Depressed/Happy/Indifferent/Sick*)

_____

_____

_____

_____

_____

_____

Did you receive a Hoover from the Narcissist today? If yes, how did you respond?

_____

_____

_____

_____

_____

List a small goal that you will work towards accomplishing tomorrow:

_____

_____

_____

_____

_____

_____

Date: ___/___/___

How are you feeling today? (Angry/*Depressed/Happy/Indifferent/Sick*)

_____

_____

_____

_____

_____

_____

Did you receive a Hoover from the Narcissist today? If yes, how did you respond?

_____

_____

_____

_____

_____

List a small goal that you will work towards accomplishing tomorrow:

_____

_____

_____

_____

_____

_____

"When a man's ways please the LORD, he maketh even his enemies to be at peace with him."
-Proverbs 16:7

"Be ye strong therefore, and let not your hands be weak: for your work shall be rewarded."

-2 Chronicles 15:7

Date: ___/___/___

How are you feeling today? (Angry/*Depressed/Happy/Indifferent/Sick*)

_____

_____

_____

_____

_____

_____

_____

Did you receive a Hoover from the Narcissist today? If yes, how did you respond?

_____

_____

_____

_____

_____

_____

List a small goal that you will work towards accomplishing tomorrow:

_____

_____

_____

_____

_____

_____

_____

Date: ___/___/___

How are you feeling today? (Angry/*Depressed/Happy/Indifferent/Sick*)

_____

_____

_____

_____

_____

_____

_____

Did you receive a Hoover from the Narcissist today? If yes, how did you respond?

_____

_____

_____

_____

_____

List a small goal that you will work towards accomplishing tomorrow:

_____

_____

_____

_____

_____

_____

Date: ___/___/___

How are you feeling today? (Angry/*Depressed/Happy/Indifferent/Sick*)

_____

_____

_____

_____

_____

_____

_____

Did you receive a Hoover from the Narcissist today? If yes, how did you respond?

_____

_____

_____

_____

_____

_____

List a small goal that you will work towards accomplishing tomorrow:

_____

_____

_____

_____

_____

_____

_____

Date: ___/___/___

How are you feeling today? (Angry/*Depressed/Happy/Indifferent/Sick*)

_____

_____

_____

_____

_____

_____

_____

Did you receive a Hoover from the Narcissist today? If yes, how did you respond?

_____

_____

_____

_____

_____

_____

List a small goal that you will work towards accomplishing tomorrow:

_____

_____

_____

_____

_____

_____

Date: ___/___/___

How are you feeling today? (Angry/*Depressed/Happy/Indifferent/Sick*)

_____

_____

_____

_____

_____

_____

Did you receive a Hoover from the Narcissist today? If yes, how did you respond?

_____

_____

_____

_____

_____

List a small goal that you will work towards accomplishing tomorrow:

_____

_____

_____

_____

_____

Date: ___/___/___

How are you feeling today? (Angry/*Depressed*/*Happy*/*Indifferent*/*Sick*)

_____

_____

_____

_____

_____

_____

_____

Did you receive a Hoover from the Narcissist today? If yes, how did you respond?

_____

_____

_____

_____

_____

_____

List a small goal that you will work towards accomplishing tomorrow:

_____

_____

_____

_____

_____

_____

Date: ___/___/___

How are you feeling today? (Angry/*Depressed*/*Happy*/*Indifferent*/*Sick*)

_____

_____

_____

_____

_____

_____

Did you receive a Hoover from the Narcissist today? If yes, how did you respond?

_____

_____

_____

_____

_____

List a small goal that you will work towards accomplishing tomorrow:

_____

_____

_____

_____

_____

Date: ___/___/___

How are you feeling today? (Angry/*Depressed/Happy/Indifferent/Sick*)

_____

_____

_____

_____

_____

_____

_____

Did you receive a Hoover from the Narcissist today? If yes, how did you respond?

_____

_____

_____

_____

_____

_____

List a small goal that you will work towards accomplishing tomorrow:

_____

_____

_____

_____

_____

_____

Date: ___/___/___

How are you feeling today? (Angry/*Depressed/Happy/Indifferent/Sick*)

_____

_____

_____

_____

_____

_____

_____

Did you receive a Hoover from the Narcissist today? If yes, how did you respond?

_____

_____

_____

_____

_____

_____

List a small goal that you will work towards accomplishing tomorrow:

_____

_____

_____

_____

_____

_____

Date: ___/___/___

How are you feeling today? (Angry/*Depressed/Happy/Indifferent/Sick*)

_____

_____

_____

_____

_____

_____

_____

Did you receive a Hoover from the Narcissist today? If yes, how did you respond?

_____

_____

_____

_____

_____

_____

List a small goal that you will work towards accomplishing tomorrow:

_____

_____

_____

_____

_____

_____

Date: ___/___/___

How are you feeling today? (Angry/*Depressed/Happy/Indifferent/Sick*)

_____

_____

_____

_____

_____

_____

Did you receive a Hoover from the Narcissist today? If yes, how did you respond?

_____

_____

_____

_____

_____

List a small goal that you will work towards accomplishing tomorrow:

_____

_____

_____

_____

_____

Date: ___/___/___

How are you feeling today? (Angry/*Depressed/Happy/Indifferent/Sick*)

_____

_____

_____

_____

_____

_____

Did you receive a Hoover from the Narcissist today? If yes, how did you respond?

_____

_____

_____

_____

_____

List a small goal that you will work towards accomplishing tomorrow:

_____

_____

_____

_____

_____

Date: ___/___/___

How are you feeling today? (Angry/*Depressed*/*Happy*/*Indifferent*/*Sick*)

_____

_____

_____

_____

_____

_____

Did you receive a Hoover from the Narcissist today? If yes, how did you respond?

_____

_____

_____

_____

_____

List a small goal that you will work towards accomplishing tomorrow:

_____

_____

_____

_____

_____

_____

Date: ___/___/___

How are you feeling today? (Angry/*Depressed*/*Happy*/*Indifferent*/*Sick*)

_____

_____

_____

_____

_____

_____

Did you receive a Hoover from the Narcissist today? If yes, how did you respond?

_____

_____

_____

_____

_____

List a small goal that you will work towards accomplishing tomorrow:

_____

_____

_____

_____

_____

Date: ___/___/___

How are you feeling today? (Angry/*Depressed/Happy/Indifferent/Sick*)

_____

_____

_____

_____

_____

_____

Did you receive a Hoover from the Narcissist today? If yes, how did you respond?

_____

_____

_____

_____

_____

List a small goal that you will work towards accomplishing tomorrow:

_____

_____

_____

_____

_____

Date: ___/___/___

How are you feeling today? (Angry/*Depressed*/*Happy*/*Indifferent*/*Sick*)

_____

_____

_____

_____

_____

_____

Did you receive a Hoover from the Narcissist today? If yes, how did you respond?

_____

_____

_____

_____

_____

List a small goal that you will work towards accomplishing tomorrow:

_____

_____

_____

_____

_____

_____

Date: ___/___/___

How are you feeling today? (Angry/*Depressed*/*Happy*/*Indifferent*/*Sick*)

_____

_____

_____

_____

_____

_____

Did you receive a Hoover from the Narcissist today? If yes, how did you respond?

_____

_____

_____

_____

_____

List a small goal that you will work towards accomplishing tomorrow:

_____

_____

_____

_____

_____

_____

Date: ___/___/___

How are you feeling today? (Angry/*Depressed/Happy/Indifferent/Sick*)

_____

_____

_____

_____

_____

_____

Did you receive a Hoover from the Narcissist today? If yes, how did you respond?

_____

_____

_____

_____

_____

List a small goal that you will work towards accomplishing tomorrow:

_____

_____

_____

_____

_____

Date: ___/___/___

How are you feeling today? (Angry/*Depressed*/*Happy*/*Indifferent*/*Sick*)

_____

_____

_____

_____

_____

_____

Did you receive a Hoover from the Narcissist today? If yes, how did you respond?

_____

_____

_____

_____

_____

List a small goal that you will work towards accomplishing tomorrow:

_____

_____

_____

_____

_____

Date: ___/___/___

How are you feeling today? (Angry/*Depressed*/*Happy*/*Indifferent*/*Sick*)

_____

_____

_____

_____

_____

_____

_____

Did you receive a Hoover from the Narcissist today? If yes, how did you respond?

_____

_____

_____

_____

_____

_____

List a small goal that you will work towards accomplishing tomorrow:

_____

_____

_____

_____

_____

Date: ___/___/___

How are you feeling today? (Angry/*Depressed/Happy/Indifferent/Sick*)

_____

_____

_____

_____

_____

_____

_____

Did you receive a Hoover from the Narcissist today? If yes, how did you respond?

_____

_____

_____

_____

_____

List a small goal that you will work towards accomplishing tomorrow:

_____

_____

_____

_____

_____

Date: ___/___/___

How are you feeling today? (Angry/*Depressed/Happy/Indifferent/Sick*)

_____

_____

_____

_____

_____

_____

_____

Did you receive a Hoover from the Narcissist today? If yes, how did you respond?

_____

_____

_____

_____

_____

_____

List a small goal that you will work towards accomplishing tomorrow:

_____

_____

_____

_____

_____

_____

Date: ___/___/___

How are you feeling today? (Angry/*Depressed*/*Happy*/*Indifferent*/*Sick*)

_____

_____

_____

_____

_____

_____

Did you receive a Hoover from the Narcissist today? If yes, how did you respond?

_____

_____

_____

_____

_____

List a small goal that you will work towards accomplishing tomorrow:

_____

_____

_____

_____

_____

Date: ___/___/___

How are you feeling today? (Angry/*Depressed/Happy/Indifferent/Sick*)

_____

_____

_____

_____

_____

_____

_____

Did you receive a Hoover from the Narcissist today? If yes, how did you respond?

_____

_____

_____

_____

_____

_____

List a small goal that you will work towards accomplishing tomorrow:

_____

_____

_____

_____

_____

_____

Date: ___/___/___

How are you feeling today? (Angry/*Depressed*/*Happy*/*Indifferent*/*Sick*)

_____

_____

_____

_____

_____

_____

Did you receive a Hoover from the Narcissist today? If yes, how did you respond?

_____

_____

_____

_____

_____

List a small goal that you will work towards accomplishing tomorrow:

_____

_____

_____

_____

_____

Date: ___/___/___

How are you feeling today? (Angry/*Depressed/Happy/Indifferent/Sick*)

_____

_____

_____

_____

_____

_____

_____

Did you receive a Hoover from the Narcissist today? If yes, how did you respond?

_____

_____

_____

_____

_____

List a small goal that you will work towards accomplishing tomorrow:

_____

_____

_____

_____

_____

Date: ___/___/___

How are you feeling today? (Angry/*Depressed*/*Happy*/*Indifferent*/*Sick*)

_____

_____

_____

_____

_____

_____

Did you receive a Hoover from the Narcissist today? If yes, how did you respond?

_____

_____

_____

_____

_____

List a small goal that you will work towards accomplishing tomorrow:

_____

_____

_____

_____

_____

Date: ___/___/___

How are you feeling today? (Angry/*Depressed/Happy/Indifferent/Sick*)

_____

_____

_____

_____

_____

_____

_____

Did you receive a Hoover from the Narcissist today? If yes, how did you respond?

_____

_____

_____

_____

_____

List a small goal that you will work towards accomplishing tomorrow:

_____

_____

_____

_____

_____

"Loving people live in a loving world. Hostile people live in a hostile world.

Same world."
-Wayne Dyer

"It does not matter how slowly you go, so long as you do not stop."
-Confucius

Date: ___/___/___

How are you feeling today? (Angry/*Depressed/Happy/Indifferent/Sick*)

_____

_____

_____

_____

_____

_____

_____

Did you receive a Hoover from the Narcissist today? If yes, how did you respond?

_____

_____

_____

_____

_____

_____

List a small goal that you will work towards accomplishing tomorrow:

_____

_____

_____

_____

_____

_____

_____

Date: ___/___/___

How are you feeling today? (Angry/*Depressed/Happy/Indifferent/Sick*)

_____

_____

_____

_____

_____

_____

_____

Did you receive a Hoover from the Narcissist today? If yes, how did you respond?

_____

_____

_____

_____

_____

_____

List a small goal that you will work towards accomplishing tomorrow:

_____

_____

_____

_____

_____

_____

Date: ___/___/___

How are you feeling today? (Angry/*Depressed/Happy/Indifferent/Sick*)

_____

_____

_____

_____

_____

_____

Did you receive a Hoover from the Narcissist today? If yes, how did you respond?

_____

_____

_____

_____

_____

List a small goal that you will work towards accomplishing tomorrow:

_____

_____

_____

_____

_____

Date: ___/___/___

How are you feeling today? (Angry/*Depressed/Happy/Indifferent/Sick*)

_____

_____

_____

_____

_____

_____

Did you receive a Hoover from the Narcissist today? If yes, how did you respond?

_____

_____

_____

_____

_____

List a small goal that you will work towards accomplishing tomorrow:

_____

_____

_____

_____

_____

Date: ___/___/___

How are you feeling today? (Angry/*Depressed*/*Happy*/*Indifferent*/*Sick*)

_____

_____

_____

_____

_____

_____

Did you receive a Hoover from the Narcissist today? If yes, how did you respond?

_____

_____

_____

_____

_____

List a small goal that you will work towards accomplishing tomorrow:

_____

_____

_____

_____

_____

_____

Date: ___/___/___

How are you feeling today? (Angry/*Depressed/Happy/Indifferent/Sick*)

Did you receive a Hoover from the Narcissist today? If yes, how did you respond?

List a small goal that you will work towards accomplishing tomorrow:

Date: ___/___/___

How are you feeling today? (Angry/*Depressed/Happy/Indifferent/Sick*)

_____

_____

_____

_____

_____

_____

_____

Did you receive a Hoover from the Narcissist today? If yes, how did you respond?

_____

_____

_____

_____

_____

List a small goal that you will work towards accomplishing tomorrow:

_____

_____

_____

_____

_____

Date: ___/___/___

How are you feeling today? (Angry/*Depressed*/*Happy*/*Indifferent*/*Sick*)

_____

_____

_____

_____

_____

_____

_____

_____

Did you receive a Hoover from the Narcissist today? If yes, how did you respond?

_____

_____

_____

_____

_____

_____

List a small goal that you will work towards accomplishing tomorrow:

_____

_____

_____

_____

_____

_____

_____

Date: ___/___/___

How are you feeling today? (Angry/*Depressed/Happy/Indifferent/Sick*)

_____

_____

_____

_____

_____

_____

Did you receive a Hoover from the Narcissist today? If yes, how did you respond?

_____

_____

_____

_____

_____

List a small goal that you will work towards accomplishing tomorrow:

_____

_____

_____

_____

_____

Date: ___/___/___

How are you feeling today? (Angry/*Depressed/Happy/Indifferent/Sick*)

_____

_____

_____

_____

_____

_____

_____

Did you receive a Hoover from the Narcissist today? If yes, how did you respond?

_____

_____

_____

_____

_____

_____

List a small goal that you will work towards accomplishing tomorrow:

_____

_____

_____

_____

_____

_____

Date: ___/___/___

How are you feeling today? (Angry/*Depressed/Happy/Indifferent/Sick*)

_____

_____

_____

_____

_____

_____

Did you receive a Hoover from the Narcissist today? If yes, how did you respond?

_____

_____

_____

_____

_____

List a small goal that you will work towards accomplishing tomorrow:

_____

_____

_____

_____

_____

Date: ___/___/___

How are you feeling today? (Angry/*Depressed*/*Happy*/*Indifferent*/*Sick*)

_____

_____

_____

_____

_____

_____

_____

Did you receive a Hoover from the Narcissist today? If yes, how did you respond?

_____

_____

_____

_____

_____

_____

List a small goal that you will work towards accomplishing tomorrow:

_____

_____

_____

_____

_____

_____

Date: ___/___/___

How are you feeling today? (Angry/*Depressed/Happy/Indifferent/Sick*)

_____

_____

_____

_____

_____

_____

_____

Did you receive a Hoover from the Narcissist today? If yes, how did you respond?

_____

_____

_____

_____

_____

_____

List a small goal that you will work towards accomplishing tomorrow:

_____

_____

_____

_____

_____

_____

Date: ___/___/___

How are you feeling today? (Angry/*Depressed/Happy/Indifferent/Sick*)

_____

_____

_____

_____

_____

_____

_____

Did you receive a Hoover from the Narcissist today? If yes, how did you respond?

_____

_____

_____

_____

_____

List a small goal that you will work towards accomplishing tomorrow:

_____

_____

_____

_____

_____

_____

Date: ___/___/___

How are you feeling today? (Angry/*Depressed/Happy/Indifferent/Sick*)

_____

_____

_____

_____

_____

_____

_____

Did you receive a Hoover from the Narcissist today? If yes, how did you respond?

_____

_____

_____

_____

_____

_____

List a small goal that you will work towards accomplishing tomorrow:

_____

_____

_____

_____

_____

_____

Date: ___/___/___

How are you feeling today? (Angry/*Depressed/Happy/Indifferent/Sick*)

_____

_____

_____

_____

_____

_____

Did you receive a Hoover from the Narcissist today? If yes, how did you respond?

_____

_____

_____

_____

_____

List a small goal that you will work towards accomplishing tomorrow:

_____

_____

_____

_____

_____

Date: ___/___/___

How are you feeling today? (Angry/*Depressed/Happy/Indifferent/Sick*)

_____

_____

_____

_____

_____

_____

_____

Did you receive a Hoover from the Narcissist today? If yes, how did you respond?

_____

_____

_____

_____

_____

_____

List a small goal that you will work towards accomplishing tomorrow:

_____

_____

_____

_____

_____

_____

_____

Date: ___/___/___

How are you feeling today? (Angry/*Depressed/Happy/Indifferent/Sick*)

_____

_____

_____

_____

_____

_____

Did you receive a Hoover from the Narcissist today? If yes, how did you respond?

_____

_____

_____

_____

_____

List a small goal that you will work towards accomplishing tomorrow:

_____

_____

_____

_____

_____

"Do not be embarrassed by your failures, learn from them and start again."
-Richard Branson

"Either you run the day or the day runs you."
-Jim Rohn

Date: ___/___/___

How are you feeling today? (Angry/*Depressed/Happy/Indifferent/Sick*)

_____

_____

_____

_____

_____

_____

Did you receive a Hoover from the Narcissist today? If yes, how did you respond?

_____

_____

_____

_____

_____

List a small goal that you will work towards accomplishing tomorrow:

_____

_____

_____

_____

_____

Date: ___/___/___

How are you feeling today? (Angry/*Depressed/Happy/Indifferent/Sick*)

_____

_____

_____

_____

_____

_____

_____

_____

Did you receive a Hoover from the Narcissist today? If yes, how did you respond?

_____

_____

_____

_____

_____

_____

List a small goal that you will work towards accomplishing tomorrow:

_____

_____

_____

_____

_____

_____

Date: ___/___/___

How are you feeling today? (Angry/*Depressed/Happy/Indifferent/Sick*)

_____

_____

_____

_____

_____

_____

_____

Did you receive a Hoover from the Narcissist today? If yes, how did you respond?

_____

_____

_____

_____

_____

_____

List a small goal that you will work towards accomplishing tomorrow:

_____

_____

_____

_____

_____

_____

Date: ___/___/___

How are you feeling today? (Angry/*Depressed*/*Happy*/*Indifferent*/*Sick*)

_____

_____

_____

_____

_____

_____

_____

Did you receive a Hoover from the Narcissist today? If yes, how did you respond?

_____

_____

_____

_____

_____

_____

List a small goal that you will work towards accomplishing tomorrow:

_____

_____

_____

_____

_____

_____

_____

Date: ___/___/___

How are you feeling today? (Angry/*Depressed*/*Happy*/*Indifferent*/*Sick*)

_____

_____

_____

_____

_____

_____

Did you receive a Hoover from the Narcissist today? If yes, how did you respond?

_____

_____

_____

_____

_____

List a small goal that you will work towards accomplishing tomorrow:

_____

_____

_____

_____

_____

_____

Date: ___/___/___

How are you feeling today? (Angry/*Depressed/Happy/Indifferent/Sick*)

_____

_____

_____

_____

_____

_____

_____

Did you receive a Hoover from the Narcissist today? If yes, how did you respond?

_____

_____

_____

_____

_____

_____

List a small goal that you will work towards accomplishing tomorrow:

_____

_____

_____

_____

_____

_____

Date: ___/___/___

How are you feeling today? (Angry/*Depressed/Happy/Indifferent/Sick*)

_____

_____

_____

_____

_____

_____

_____

Did you receive a Hoover from the Narcissist today? If yes, how did you respond?

_____

_____

_____

_____

_____

_____

List a small goal that you will work towards accomplishing tomorrow:

_____

_____

_____

_____

_____

_____

Date: ___/___/___

How are you feeling today? (Angry/*Depressed*/*Happy*/*Indifferent*/*Sick*)

_____

_____

_____

_____

_____

_____

_____

Did you receive a Hoover from the Narcissist today? If yes, how did you respond?

_____

_____

_____

_____

_____

_____

List a small goal that you will work towards accomplishing tomorrow:

_____

_____

_____

_____

_____

_____

Date: ___/___/___

How are you feeling today? (Angry/*Depressed/Happy/Indifferent/Sick*)

_____

_____

_____

_____

_____

_____

_____

Did you receive a Hoover from the Narcissist today? If yes, how did you respond?

_____

_____

_____

_____

_____

_____

List a small goal that you will work towards accomplishing tomorrow:

_____

_____

_____

_____

_____

_____

Date: ___/___/___

How are you feeling today? (Angry/*Depressed/Happy/Indifferent/Sick*)

_____

_____

_____

_____

_____

_____

_____

Did you receive a Hoover from the Narcissist today? If yes, how did you respond?

_____

_____

_____

_____

_____

List a small goal that you will work towards accomplishing tomorrow:

_____

_____

_____

_____

_____

Date: ___/___/___

How are you feeling today? (Angry/*Depressed/Happy/Indifferent/Sick*)

_____

_____

_____

_____

_____

_____

Did you receive a Hoover from the Narcissist today? If yes, how did you respond?

_____

_____

_____

_____

_____

List a small goal that you will work towards accomplishing tomorrow:

_____

_____

_____

_____

_____

Date: ___/___/___

How are you feeling today? (Angry/*Depressed/Happy/Indifferent/Sick*)

_____

_____

_____

_____

_____

_____

Did you receive a Hoover from the Narcissist today? If yes, how did you respond?

_____

_____

_____

_____

_____

List a small goal that you will work towards accomplishing tomorrow:

_____

_____

_____

_____

_____

Date: ___/___/___

How are you feeling today? (Angry/*Depressed/Happy/Indifferent/Sick*)

_____
_____
_____
_____
_____
_____
_____

Did you receive a Hoover from the Narcissist today? If yes, how did you respond?

_____
_____
_____
_____
_____
_____

List a small goal that you will work towards accomplishing tomorrow:

_____
_____
_____
_____
_____
_____

Date: ___/___/___

How are you feeling today? (Angry/*Depressed/Happy/Indifferent/Sick*)

_____

_____

_____

_____

_____

_____

_____

Did you receive a Hoover from the Narcissist today? If yes, how did you respond?

_____

_____

_____

_____

_____

_____

List a small goal that you will work towards accomplishing tomorrow:

_____

_____

_____

_____

_____

_____

Date: ___/___/___

How are you feeling today? (Angry/*Depressed/Happy/Indifferent/Sick*)

_____

_____

_____

_____

_____

_____

Did you receive a Hoover from the Narcissist today? If yes, how did you respond?

_____

_____

_____

_____

_____

List a small goal that you will work towards accomplishing tomorrow:

_____

_____

_____

_____

_____

_____

Date: ___/___/___

How are you feeling today? (Angry/*Depressed*/*Happy*/*Indifferent*/*Sick*)

_____

_____

_____

_____

_____

_____

Did you receive a Hoover from the Narcissist today? If yes, how did you respond?

_____

_____

_____

_____

_____

_____

List a small goal that you will work towards accomplishing tomorrow:

_____

_____

_____

_____

_____

_____

Date: ___/___/___

How are you feeling today? (Angry/*Depressed/Happy/Indifferent/Sick*)

_____

_____

_____

_____

_____

_____

Did you receive a Hoover from the Narcissist today? If yes, how did you respond?

_____

_____

_____

_____

_____

List a small goal that you will work towards accomplishing tomorrow:

_____

_____

_____

_____

_____

Date: ___/___/___

How are you feeling today? (Angry/*Depressed*/*Happy*/*Indifferent*/*Sick*)

_____

_____

_____

_____

_____

_____

_____

Did you receive a Hoover from the Narcissist today? If yes, how did you respond?

_____

_____

_____

_____

_____

List a small goal that you will work towards accomplishing tomorrow:

_____

_____

_____

_____

_____

_____

Date: ___/___/___

How are you feeling today? (Angry/*Depressed/Happy/Indifferent/Sick*)

_____

_____

_____

_____

_____

_____

_____

Did you receive a Hoover from the Narcissist today? If yes, how did you respond?

_____

_____

_____

_____

_____

_____

List a small goal that you will work towards accomplishing tomorrow:

_____

_____

_____

_____

_____

_____

Date: ___/___/___

How are you feeling today? (Angry/*Depressed*/*Happy*/*Indifferent*/*Sick*)

_____

_____

_____

_____

_____

_____

_____

Did you receive a Hoover from the Narcissist today? If yes, how did you respond?

_____

_____

_____

_____

_____

_____

List a small goal that you will work towards accomplishing tomorrow:

_____

_____

_____

_____

_____

_____

Date: ___/___/___

How are you feeling today? (Angry/*Depressed/Happy/Indifferent/Sick*)

_____

_____

_____

_____

_____

_____

_____

Did you receive a Hoover from the Narcissist today? If yes, how did you respond?

_____

_____

_____

_____

_____

_____

List a small goal that you will work towards accomplishing tomorrow:

_____

_____

_____

_____

_____

_____

_____

Date: ___/___/___

How are you feeling today? (Angry/*Depressed/Happy/Indifferent/Sick*)

_____

_____

_____

_____

_____

_____

_____

Did you receive a Hoover from the Narcissist today? If yes, how did you respond?

_____

_____

_____

_____

_____

List a small goal that you will work towards accomplishing tomorrow:

_____

_____

_____

_____

_____

_____

Date: ___/___/___

How are you feeling today? (Angry/*Depressed*/*Happy*/*Indifferent*/*Sick*)

_____

_____

_____

_____

_____

_____

Did you receive a Hoover from the Narcissist today? If yes, how did you respond?

_____

_____

_____

_____

_____

List a small goal that you will work towards accomplishing tomorrow:

_____

_____

_____

_____

_____

Date: ___/___/___

How are you feeling today? (Angry/*Depressed/Happy/Indifferent/Sick*)

_____

_____

_____

_____

_____

_____

Did you receive a Hoover from the Narcissist today? If yes, how did you respond?

_____

_____

_____

_____

_____

List a small goal that you will work towards accomplishing tomorrow:

_____

_____

_____

_____

_____

Date: ___/___/___

How are you feeling today? (Angry/*Depressed*/*Happy*/*Indifferent*/*Sick*)

_____

_____

_____

_____

_____

_____

_____

Did you receive a Hoover from the Narcissist today? If yes, how did you respond?

_____

_____

_____

_____

_____

_____

List a small goal that you will work towards accomplishing tomorrow:

_____

_____

_____

_____

_____

_____

Date: ___/___/___

How are you feeling today? (Angry/*Depressed/Happy/Indifferent/Sick*)

_____

_____

_____

_____

_____

_____

Did you receive a Hoover from the Narcissist today? If yes, how did you respond?

_____

_____

_____

_____

_____

List a small goal that you will work towards accomplishing tomorrow:

_____

_____

_____

_____

_____

"The best way to succeed in this world is to act on the advice you give to others."
-Unknown

"You can complain because roses have thorns, or you can rejoice because thorns have roses."
-Tom Wilson

Date: ___/___/___

How are you feeling today? (Angry/*Depressed/Happy/Indifferent/Sick*)

_____

_____

_____

_____

_____

_____

Did you receive a Hoover from the Narcissist today? If yes, how did you respond?

_____

_____

_____

_____

_____

List a small goal that you will work towards accomplishing tomorrow:

_____

_____

_____

_____

_____

_____

Date: ___/___/___

How are you feeling today? (Angry/*Depressed/Happy/Indifferent/Sick*)

_____

_____

_____

_____

_____

_____

Did you receive a Hoover from the Narcissist today? If yes, how did you respond?

_____

_____

_____

_____

_____

List a small goal that you will work towards accomplishing tomorrow:

_____

_____

_____

_____

_____

Date: ___/___/___

How are you feeling today? (Angry/*Depressed*/*Happy*/*Indifferent*/*Sick*)

_____

_____

_____

_____

_____

_____

Did you receive a Hoover from the Narcissist today? If yes, how did you respond?

_____

_____

_____

_____

_____

List a small goal that you will work towards accomplishing tomorrow:

_____

_____

_____

_____

_____

_____

Date: ___/___/___

How are you feeling today? (Angry/*Depressed*/*Happy*/*Indifferent*/*Sick*)

_____

_____

_____

_____

_____

_____

_____

Did you receive a Hoover from the Narcissist today? If yes, how did you respond?

_____

_____

_____

_____

_____

_____

List a small goal that you will work towards accomplishing tomorrow:

_____

_____

_____

_____

_____

_____

Date: ___/___/___

How are you feeling today? (Angry/*Depressed/Happy/Indifferent/Sick*)

_____

_____

_____

_____

_____

_____

_____

Did you receive a Hoover from the Narcissist today? If yes, how did you respond?

_____

_____

_____

_____

_____

_____

List a small goal that you will work towards accomplishing tomorrow:

_____

_____

_____

_____

_____

_____

Date: ___/___/___

How are you feeling today? (Angry/*Depressed/Happy/Indifferent/Sick*)

_____

_____

_____

_____

_____

_____

_____

Did you receive a Hoover from the Narcissist today? If yes, how did you respond?

_____

_____

_____

_____

_____

_____

List a small goal that you will work towards accomplishing tomorrow:

_____

_____

_____

_____

_____

_____

Date: ___/___/___

How are you feeling today? (Angry/*Depressed/Happy/Indifferent/Sick*)

_____

_____

_____

_____

_____

_____

_____

Did you receive a Hoover from the Narcissist today? If yes, how did you respond?

_____

_____

_____

_____

_____

_____

List a small goal that you will work towards accomplishing tomorrow:

_____

_____

_____

_____

_____

_____

Date: ___/___/___

How are you feeling today? (Angry/*Depressed/Happy/Indifferent/Sick*)

_____

_____

_____

_____

_____

_____

_____

Did you receive a Hoover from the Narcissist today? If yes, how did you respond?

_____

_____

_____

_____

_____

List a small goal that you will work towards accomplishing tomorrow:

_____

_____

_____

_____

_____

_____

Date: ___/___/___

How are you feeling today? (Angry/*Depressed/Happy/Indifferent/Sick*)

_____

_____

_____

_____

_____

_____

_____

Did you receive a Hoover from the Narcissist today? If yes, how did you respond?

_____

_____

_____

_____

_____

_____

List a small goal that you will work towards accomplishing tomorrow:

_____

_____

_____

_____

_____

_____

Date: ___/___/___

How are you feeling today? (Angry/*Depressed/Happy/Indifferent/Sick*)

_____

_____

_____

_____

_____

_____

Did you receive a Hoover from the Narcissist today? If yes, how did you respond?

_____

_____

_____

_____

_____

_____

List a small goal that you will work towards accomplishing tomorrow:

_____

_____

_____

_____

_____

_____

_____

Date: ___/___/___

How are you feeling today? (Angry/*Depressed/Happy/Indifferent/Sick*)

_____

_____

_____

_____

_____

_____

Did you receive a Hoover from the Narcissist today? If yes, how did you respond?

_____

_____

_____

_____

_____

List a small goal that you will work towards accomplishing tomorrow:

_____

_____

_____

_____

_____

Date: ___/___/___

How are you feeling today? (Angry/*Depressed*/*Happy*/*Indifferent*/*Sick*)

_____

_____

_____

_____

_____

_____

_____

Did you receive a Hoover from the Narcissist today? If yes, how did you respond?

_____

_____

_____

_____

_____

_____

List a small goal that you will work towards accomplishing tomorrow:

_____

_____

_____

_____

_____

_____

Date: ___/___/___

How are you feeling today? (Angry/*Depressed*/*Happy*/*Indifferent*/*Sick*)

_____

_____

_____

_____

_____

_____

_____

Did you receive a Hoover from the Narcissist today? If yes, how did you respond?

_____

_____

_____

_____

_____

_____

List a small goal that you will work towards accomplishing tomorrow:

_____

_____

_____

_____

_____

_____

Date: ___/___/___

How are you feeling today? (Angry/*Depressed/Happy/Indifferent/Sick*)

_____

_____

_____

_____

_____

_____

Did you receive a Hoover from the Narcissist today? If yes, how did you respond?

_____

_____

_____

_____

_____

_____

List a small goal that you will work towards accomplishing tomorrow:

_____

_____

_____

_____

_____

_____

Date: ___/___/___

How are you feeling today? (Angry/*Depressed/Happy/Indifferent/Sick*)

_____

_____

_____

_____

_____

_____

Did you receive a Hoover from the Narcissist today? If yes, how did you respond?

_____

_____

_____

_____

_____

List a small goal that you will work towards accomplishing tomorrow:

_____

_____

_____

_____

_____

Date: ___/___/___

How are you feeling today? (Angry/*Depressed*/*Happy*/*Indifferent*/*Sick*)

_____

_____

_____

_____

_____

_____

Did you receive a Hoover from the Narcissist today? If yes, how did you respond?

_____

_____

_____

_____

_____

List a small goal that you will work towards accomplishing tomorrow:

_____

_____

_____

_____

_____

Date: ___/___/___

How are you feeling today? (Angry/*Depressed/Happy/Indifferent/Sick*)

_____

_____

_____

_____

_____

_____

_____

Did you receive a Hoover from the Narcissist today? If yes, how did you respond?

_____

_____

_____

_____

_____

_____

List a small goal that you will work towards accomplishing tomorrow:

_____

_____

_____

_____

_____

_____

Date: ___/___/___

How are you feeling today? (Angry/*Depressed/Happy/Indifferent/Sick*)

_____

_____

_____

_____

_____

_____

Did you receive a Hoover from the Narcissist today? If yes, how did you respond?

_____

_____

_____

_____

_____

List a small goal that you will work towards accomplishing tomorrow:

_____

_____

_____

_____

_____

_____

Date: ___/___/___

How are you feeling today? (Angry/*Depressed/Happy/Indifferent/Sick*)

_____

_____

_____

_____

_____

_____

Did you receive a Hoover from the Narcissist today? If yes, how did you respond?

_____

_____

_____

_____

_____

List a small goal that you will work towards accomplishing tomorrow:

_____

_____

_____

_____

_____

Date: ___/___/___

How are you feeling today? (Angry/*Depressed/Happy/Indifferent/Sick*)

_____

_____

_____

_____

_____

_____

_____

Did you receive a Hoover from the Narcissist today? If yes, how did you respond?

_____

_____

_____

_____

_____

_____

List a small goal that you will work towards accomplishing tomorrow:

_____

_____

_____

_____

_____

_____

Date: ___/___/___

How are you feeling today? (Angry/*Depressed*/*Happy*/*Indifferent*/*Sick*)

_____

_____

_____

_____

_____

_____

Did you receive a Hoover from the Narcissist today? If yes, how did you respond?

_____

_____

_____

_____

_____

List a small goal that you will work towards accomplishing tomorrow:

_____

_____

_____

_____

_____

_____

Date: ___/___/___

How are you feeling today? (Angry/*Depressed/Happy/Indifferent/Sick*)

_____

_____

_____

_____

_____

_____

_____

Did you receive a Hoover from the Narcissist today? If yes, how did you respond?

_____

_____

_____

_____

_____

_____

List a small goal that you will work towards accomplishing tomorrow:

_____

_____

_____

_____

_____

_____

Date: ___/___/___

How are you feeling today? (Angry/*Depressed*/*Happy*/*Indifferent*/*Sick*)

_____

_____

_____

_____

_____

_____

_____

Did you receive a Hoover from the Narcissist today? If yes, how did you respond?

_____

_____

_____

_____

_____

_____

List a small goal that you will work towards accomplishing tomorrow:

_____

_____

_____

_____

_____

_____

Date: ___/___/___

How are you feeling today? (Angry/*Depressed/Happy/Indifferent/Sick*)

_____

_____

_____

_____

_____

_____

_____

Did you receive a Hoover from the Narcissist today? If yes, how did you respond?

_____

_____

_____

_____

_____

_____

List a small goal that you will work towards accomplishing tomorrow:

_____

_____

_____

_____

_____

_____

Date: ___/___/___

How are you feeling today? (Angry/*Depressed/Happy/Indifferent/Sick*)

_____

_____

_____

_____

_____

_____

_____

Did you receive a Hoover from the Narcissist today? If yes, how did you respond?

_____

_____

_____

_____

_____

_____

List a small goal that you will work towards accomplishing tomorrow:

_____

_____

_____

_____

_____

_____

"No act of kindness,
no matter how small,
is ever wasted."
-Aesop

"No one can make you feel inferior without your consent."
-Eleanor Roosevelt

Made in the USA
Las Vegas, NV
21 June 2022